Hip Knit Hats

Hip Knit Hats

40 Fabulous Designs

CATHY CARRON

LARK BOOKS

A Division of Sterling Publishing Co., Inc.
New York / London

DEDICATION

To Andy

Editor: **Joanne O'Sullivan**

Art Director: **Dana M. Irwin**

Cover Designer: **Barbara Zaretsky**

Photography: **Sandra Stambaugh**
(model photography)

Sean Moser
(how-to photography)

www.keithwright.com
(cover photography, hat photography,
special photography pages 19, 109, 116, 120)

Illustrations: **August Hoerr** (pages 28, 29)
Dana Irwin (pages 30, 31)
Orrin Lundgren (page 28)

Associate Art Director: **Shannon Yokeley**

Assistant Art Director: **Lance Wille**

Editorial Assistance: **Delores Gosnell**

Library of Congress Cataloging-in-Publication Data

Carron, Cathy.
  Hip knit hats : 40 fabulous designs / by Cathy Carron.
      p. cm.
  Includes bibliographical references and index.
  ISBN 1-57990-644-3 (hardcover)
  1. Knitting--Patterns. 2. Hats. I. Title.
TT825.C232 2005
746.43'204322--dc22

                                            2005008137

10 9 8 7

Published by Lark Books, A Division of
Sterling Publishing Co., Inc.
387 Park Avenue South, New York, N.Y. 10016

Text © 2005, Cathy Carron
Photography © 2005, Lark Books
Illustrations © 2005, Lark Books

Distributed in Canada by Sterling Publishing,
c/o Canadian Manda Group, 165 Dufferin Street
Toronto, Ontario, Canada M6K 3H6

Distributed in the United Kingdom by GMC Distribution Services,
Castle Place, 166 High Street, Lewes, East Sussex, England BN7 1XU

Distributed in Australia by Capricorn Link (Australia) Pty Ltd.,
P.O. Box 704, Windsor, NSW 2756 Australia

If you have questions or comments about this book,
please contact:
Lark Books
67 Broadway, Asheville, NC 28801
(828) 253-0467

Manufactured in China

ISBN 13: 978-1-57990-644-3
ISBN 10: 1-57990-644-3

For information about custom editions, special sales, premium and
corporate purchases, please contact Sterling Special Sales Department
at 800-805-5489 or specialsales@sterlingpub.com.

CONTENTS

INTRODUCTION

NEEDLES POISED!

THIS COLLECTION OF KNITTED HAT PATTERNS

sprang from my head in more ways than one. It all started because of my larger-than-average head size. The average head circumference measures about 21 inches (53 cm), yet mine is a generous 23 inches (58 cm). On the other hand, I know there are people who describe themselves as "pinheads." Spring and summer straw hats are often available in a range of sizes, but knit hatmakers tend to cling stubbornly to the outdated notion that one-size-fits-all. You might be able to pull one on, but getting it off is quite another story. This collection offers two sizes—medium and large—which should instantly cure "squished head syndrome," and the most severe cases of hat hair, which occurs when a hat fits so tightly that it makes your head sweat and your hair frizz up. My mantra is "Knit to Fit!"

With 40 patterns, and nearly 100 variations in all, you're bound to find a hat that perfectly fits, not only your head, but also your wardrobe. These hip hats are as much about style as they are about warmth and comfort. They're great accessories to wear and be seen in, even when you're not having a bad hair day!

The first section of the book will take you through the basics of hat construction, introducing you to knitting in-the-round and working with double-pointed and circular needles. We'll review traditional methods of casting on, and I'll present a technique I call the Wrap Method, which you'll find useful for hatmaking. Although these techniques may seem challenging to the uninitiated, once you've got the hang of them, you'll find this type of knitting fun, and your results impressive.

Please pay special attention to the knitting terms and abbreviations in the chart on page 10, noting in particular how to make the proper increases.

Next, we'll delve into every knitter's passion: yarn. You'll find suggestions for how to use multiple strands of yarn to create a yarn mix, suggestions for maximizing the potential of your yarn stash, and some advice on ascertaining gauge and choosing yarn.

If you've never tried felting or fulling before, take a look at the section devoted to these fun and interesting techniques. You'll enjoy experimenting with different hat styles and discovering the effect that a cycle or two in the washing machine can have on your knitted hat.

Those who want just a little bit more detail and pizzazz in their hats will find suggestions on how to ornament and embellish their creations, including adding beads, pompoms, or tassels.

Once your hat is done, how do you wear it? You'll find an informative guide on choosing a hat style that flatters in the Picking a Hat Style section.

Finally, the patterns! This varied collection of hats—casual and chic, with a bit of cheek—focuses on great basic shapes that can be fashioned to complement any jacket or coat. I named the hats after people (real and fictional) who inspired them or who I could imagine wearing them. There is truly something for everyone, young and old, sporty or stylish, women and men alike. Make your old favorite standby, or be fearless and try a new range of styles. You might be pleasantly surprised at how many different looks you can successfully wear.

It has been great fun working through these designs, and I hope you'll enjoy making them as much as I do.

HAT CONSTRUCTION AND KNITTING TECHNIQUES

KNITTED HATS CAN BE MADE IN MYRIAD WAYS,
the only limit being your imagination. They can be knitted as a whole, knitted in pieces and patched together, or knitted sideways and seamed together. But for our purposes (making standard shapes), most of the instructions in this book call for making a hat in one piece, either from the brim upward or from the crown downward.

Many (if not most) of the hat patterns in this collection specify top-down construction, which means that you will begin making the hat starting at the very center of the crown. As you knit, regular and periodic increases are made that multiply the number of stitches and expand the crown as required to meet the head circumference for an easy fit. That means that you will need to start with a set of four double-pointed needles (dpn). As the number of stitches increases, you can switch over to a circular needle (cn) or continue to knit it entirely on double-pointed needles.

All top-down hats begin with 12 stitches, which can be cast on in a number of different ways. The Wrap Method, described on page 14, is one that I highly recommend because it's fun to do and creates a holeless crown as well. It works especially well for felted hats, because the felting makes the starting stitches disappear into the hat entirely.

Bottom-Up
Construction

Top-Down
Construction

Hats knit from the bottom up are different. You start out with a large number of stitches to create the brim, then decrease to achieve the shaping of the crown. Top-down and bottom-up methods are essentially the same process in reverse. However, for sizing and shaping, the top-down method is preferable because if you make a mistake, want to customize the hat, or make its rise longer for some reason, you won't have to tear apart the entire hat to do so.

KNITTING IN-THE-ROUND

The optimal way to fashion a classic knitted hat is without seams, which means knitting in-the-round. Seamless knitting provides the best appearance and fit. Except for hats with irregular tops (referred to in this book as Witty Knits), most of the other styles are knitted from the top down using double-pointed needles (dpn) and then circular needles (cn) as the stitches multiply.

Mastering double-pointed needles (dpn) and circular needles (cn) is the biggest challenge for any would-be hatmaker. The good news is that it's not really difficult at all. In fact, it's lots of fun once you get the hang of it. The general idea is that you're knitting stitches off one needle and onto another, repeating the process as you go around.

If you haven't knitted with double-pointed needles before, practice and do a few trial runs before you begin to make your first hat.

PATTERN ABBREVIATIONS

b   back

beg   beginning

BO   bind off

CO   cast on

cont   continue

cn   circular needle

dec   decrease

dpn   double-pointed needle(s)

f   front

inc   increase

k   knit

ktbl   knit through the back loop

k2tog   knit two stitches together

MB   make a bobble

m1   increase; make a stitch by knitting into the back of a stitch and then knitting the stitch itself

p   purl

p2tog   purl two stitches together

pm   place marker

PU   pick up

rnd   round

RS   right side

s1   slip one stitch knitwise if following stitch is knit stitch, or purlwise if following stitch is purl stitch

skp   slip 1, knit 1, pass slip stitch over

t1   increase; make a stitch by pulling up a stitch from between the two stitches in the row below

WS   wrong side

yo   yarn over

KNITTING IN-THE-ROUND

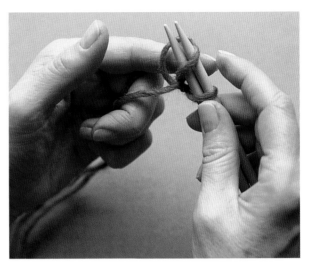

SETTING UP

Holding the two dpn together, CO 24 sts. Holding them together allows the first row to be cast on evenly and with room to knit the next row. Once you have 24 sts, slip one needle out so that now you have a loosely cast on set of sts. Without twisting the needles or stitches, divide the 24 sts amongst 3 needles, 8 sts on each needle.

KNITTING STS ONTO THE FIRST DPN

With a dpn, knit 8 sts off the first needle.

KNITTING STS ONTO THE SECOND DPN

With the free needle, knit the next 8 sts off the first needle.

KNITTING STS ONTO THE THIRD DPN

With the free needle, knit the final 8 sts off the first needle.

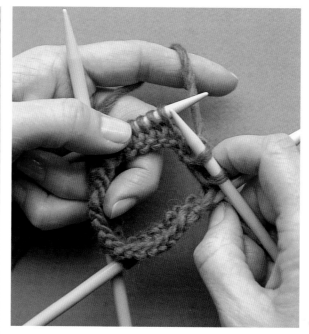

ARRANGING THE NEEDLES TO WORK IN-THE-ROUND

The 24 sts should now be evenly divided among 3 dpns. With the free needle, begin to knit the 8 sts off of the first needle, at the same time connecting the third needle with the first. So, you are now knitting "in-the-round" (rnd) instead of in rows.

MEASUREMENTS AND EQUIVALENTS

English	Metric
in inch = 2.54cm	cm centimeter = .40in
yd yards = 36in = .91m	m meter = 100cm = 39.35yd
oz ounces = 30g	g gram = .03oz

CASTING ON: TRADITIONAL METHOD I

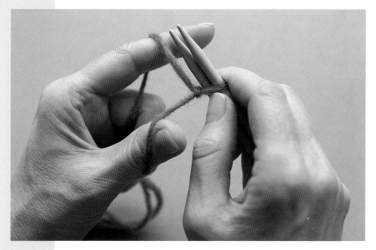

SETUP FOR CASTING ON

Measure off 1 inch/3cm of yarn for every st that you want to cast on. For 12 sts, you want to measure off at least 12 inches/30 cm of yarn plus a few extra. Make a slip knot at this junction and place on two needles being held together. Slip your thumb and index finger through the doubled-up strand of yarn created by the slip knot.

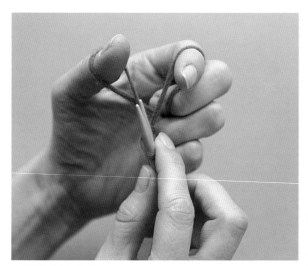

ARRANGING THE YARN ON YOUR HANDS TO BEGIN CASTING ON

Holding both sides of the yarn with your left baby finger for tension, draw your hand back to begin casting on stitches.

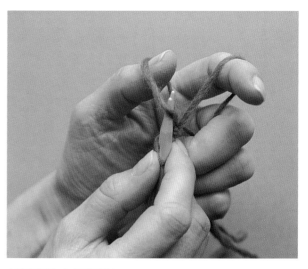

MAKING A STITCH

Slip a dpn under the thread farthest to the left and grab the left-side thread positioned on the index finger.

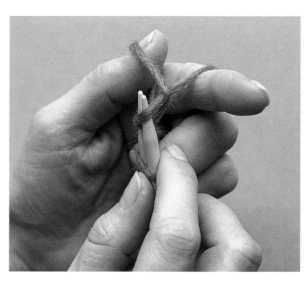

COMPLETING THE STITCH, PART I

Pull this thread under and through the first thread, then slide this st onto the right-hand needle. Repeat until you have 12 sts.

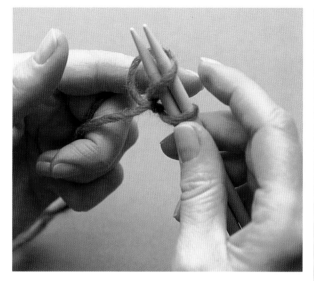

COMPLETING THE STITCH, PART II

To avoid unnecessary loops or gaps in your first row, make sure each new stitch is pulled firmly before you begin the next cast-on stitch.

SETUP FOR KNITTING IN-THE-ROUND

Once you have 12 sts, divide them among three dpn and begin to knit in-the-round.

CASTING ON: TRADITIONAL METHOD II

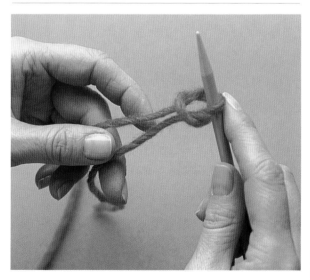

SETUP FOR CASTING ON

Make a simple loop stitch or slipknot.

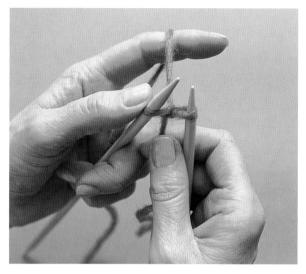

MAKING A STITCH

Knit into the loop stitch.

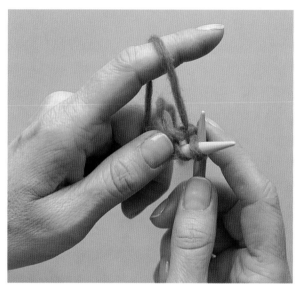

TRANSFERING THE STITCH

Place that stitch on the right-hand needle. Repeat until there are 12 sts.

KNITTING IN-THE-ROUND

Divide the 12 sts among three dpn and knit 1 rnd. Continue by following the pattern instructions.

CASTING ON: THE WRAP METHOD

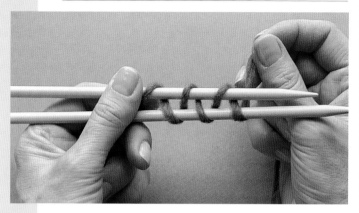

STARTING THE WRAP, PART I

Holding the two dpns together and starting from the left, wrap the yarn around the needles as shown.

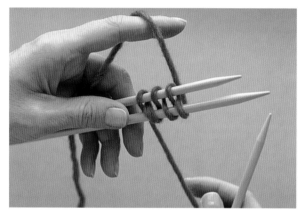

STARTING THE WRAP, PART II

You should have three "wraps" or sts, on each side.

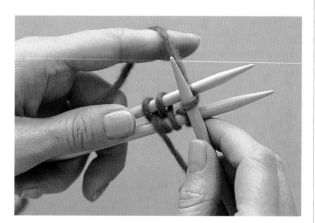

TRANSFERING THE STITCHES

Using the third needle, knit the 3 sts on the left needle, turn the work and using another needle, knit the 3 sts on that side.

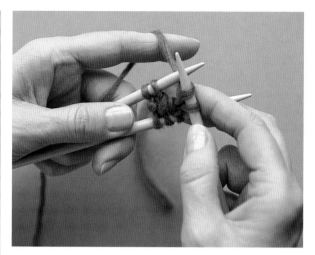

STARTING INCREASES

Next round, with a free dpn, increase 1 st in each of the next 2 sts. Using another free dpn, repeat. Using the third and last dpn, repeat. When the round is completed, you should have 4 sts on each of three dpn for a total of 12 sts.

K 1 rnd.

MAKING INCREASES

For the next round, k1, inc 1 st in the next st and repeat around.

K 1 rnd.

Next rnd, k2, inc 1 st in the next st, repeat around. K 1 round. Repeat this pattern, increasing by 1 additional st between increases, until you have increased the crown to the desired diameter or size. Once all increases have been completed, knit the sts onto a cn for medium size (16"/41cm) or large size (24"/61cm); small size hats have to be completed on dpn.

INCREASING STITCHES

Increasing and decreasing stitches shapes the knitted piece you're making. There's more than one way to increase the number of stitches on your needle. This section focuses on increasing, rather than decreasing because of the top-down construction of many of the patterns in the book. You'll be multiplying stitches to obtain the proper head circumference. You might ask, "Why do I need to know more than one way to increase?" The answer is that each method creates a different appearance in the finished knitted piece. For instance, a yarnover (yo) increase leaves holes, which is why this kind of increase is commonly used in lacemaking. Pulling a stitch from behind the next one to be worked on the needle has the opposite effect. You'll need to make increases exactly as specified in a pattern in order to achieve the desired effect.

YARNOVERS (YO)

This method involves bringing the yarn forward and over the right-hand needle, thereby placing another stitch on the needle. The stitch immediately following is then knitted or purled, securing the yarnover in its place. Yarnovers are most often used for mesh or lacemaking, but they are also needed for picot edgings and to create spaces to run ribbon or a string through a knitted piece.

TAKE ONE (T1)

For this increase, slip the right-hand needle between the two sts in the row below, and pull up 1 st, placing it on the right-hand needle. This also creates a hole, but usually not as large as a yo.

MAKE ONE (M1)

This increase involves knitting in the back of the st on the left-hand needle, and then knitting the stitch itself, creating an almost invisible increase (i.e., no hole).

FINISHING

After you have finished knitting your hat, you will have yarn ends hanging out. One at a time, thread each end onto a needle and then work it into the back of the fabric, ideally for 2 inches/5 cm.

If you have not used the Wrap Method to cast on at the beginning, but instead cast on 12 sts in one of the more traditional ways, you will also need to secure the hole that was made.

To do this, thread a darning needle with the yarn end, and take a stitch in each loop around. Once you have gone all the way around, pull firmly and push the needle through to the wrong side and secure inside, drawing the thread through the fabric for 1 to 2 inches/2.4 to 5cm.

Yarn and Gauge

Knitted hats can be made with just about any yarn weight, but this collection relies primarily on heavier weight yarns that produce fewer stitches per inch. With heavier yarn, hats knit up more quickly, but more important, the weight of the yarn offers more heft and, therefore, more shape to the hat.

Using Multiple Strands of Yarns

Instead of using yarn right off the skein, try creating a yarn mix to achieve the same gauge specified in the project instructions. Using multiple strands of different colors of yarn or shades of a single color instantly creates new and unique textures that can give a hat a whole new dimension. Best of all, you get a one-of-a-kind look.

Before you buy your yarn, check your own stash of leftover skeins and balls first. Experiment and play with various combinations and mixes. You might be able to come up with a creation made completely out of scraps, but if not, don't be shy about supplementing what you have with a great new ball of something wonderful in your local yarn shop. Here are a few design tips:

◆ Create a "tonal" hat by using strands in the same color family—for example, cool blues and greens, hot reds and oranges, or even neutral browns and grays.

◆ Stretch your leftover yarn supply—if you have a substantial amount of yarn in a certain color, but not quite enough, put a stripe in the hat. The stripe can be broad (see Jesse, page 34) or the stripe can be the entire brim (see Mari, page 55). Adding embellishments, such as pompoms, fringe, tassels, beadwork, or even embroidered designs made with leftovers, can provide the unique look you seek.

Whether you intend to use scraps or head out to the yarn shop, it might help to envision, sketch, or describe the hat you would love to make. On the flip side, look at the yarns first and become inspired! There are infinite ways to get the creative juices flowing.

Mix it Up by Blending Yarns

Yarn weight	Gauge (sts per in)	Needles	Yarn Combinations and Approximate Equivalents
Fingering	7/18 cm	#0 to #4	———
Sport	6/15 cm	#5 or #6	2 fingering
Worsted	5/13 cm	#7 or #8	2 sport OR 1 sport and 2 fingering
Heavy Worsted	4 to 4½/ 10 to 11.5 cm	#8 or #9	3 sport OR 1 sport and 1 worsted
Chunky	3 to 3½/ 7.5 to 9 cm	#10	1 heavy worsted and worsted OR 1 worsted and 2 or 3 sport
Bulky	2 to ½/ 5 to 6.5 cm	#10½ or #11 or even larger!	3 worsted OR 1 mohair and 1 chunky OR 1 chunky and 1 worsted OR 1 thick chenille

MAKE SWATCHES TO ASCERTAIN GAUGE

Establishing the proper gauge for the pattern is of the utmost importance. This is even more so for hats than for garments, because if you are 1 inch/2.5cm or so off, you'll either be wearing the hat down around your nose, or worse yet, you might not even be able to get it on. If, after making a swatch, you have too many stitches per inch using the needles specified, you will have to increase the needle size. Conversely, if there are too few stitches per inch for the needle specified, try a smaller needle.

Start the hat only when you have figured out the combination of needles and yarn that will give you the proper gauge. Use the chart on page 16 as a guideline for the approximate needle size that each weight of yarn requires. The chart indicates the gauge range used for this pattern collection, but it doesn't take into account your own personal knitting style, or your tension and the resulting gauge, which in the end is why swatchmaking is a must.

YARN TYPES

Just because a yarn is labeled worsted or sport doesn't necessarily make it so. Most companies try to stay within certain guidelines for categorizing a yarn, but then again there is no yarn "bureau of standards" and you are left on your own to determine the actual weight. This is especially true for novelty yarns. However, in no way should you walk away from the mystery ball that is dazzling your eyes and fingers because you're not sure of what to call it or do with it!

The only thing that should matter to you about any fiber is what gauge it will give you in the end.

If you are really unsure, try it and make a swatch, or ask the salesperson—many stores have swatches already prepared. DK weight yarns are often the most difficult to determine—some knit up like a sport yarn and others as worsteds. Again, check the gauge.

And finally, don't pass up an interesting ball of yarn because it appears too thin (i.e, it has a small gauge). Consider blending it into a mix of yarns using the chart on page 16 to get the gauge your pattern requires. It's lots of fun, and often the results are unexpectedly pleasing.

THE ART OF FELTING & FULLING

Fulling and felting are two similar processes by which knitted fabric is treated with heat, moisture, and pressure to shrink and thicken it, transforming its texture entirely. Fulling creates a matted material that doesn't necessarily obscure the underlying structure of the knit or weave, whereas felting compresses the fibers to create a smoother, and perhaps even more rigid material. Fabric that has been felted or fulled becomes denser and more capable of retaining heat and keeping out the elements than plain knitted or unfelted garments.

Felting is relatively easy. Witnessing the transformation of something you have made into another form entirely is exciting and fun. There's just one thing to keep in the back of your mind while you go through the various steps: Felting is more of an art than an exact science. The highly individualized nature of various yarns and fibers on the market today make it even more so. The two most important factors affecting the outcome of your project will be the type and quality of the yarn you use and the performance of your washing machine, particularly the temperature of the hot water setting.

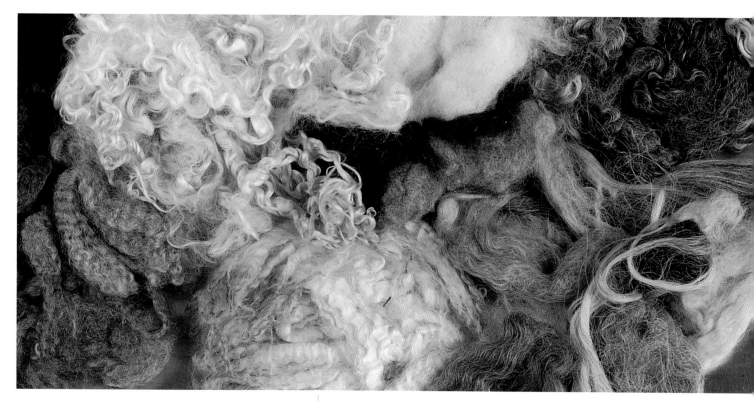

Yarn

When felting, it's essential that the yarn used to make your hat consists mostly of wool; 100% wool content is best, but interesting results can also be achieved when wool is 85 to 99% wool. Wool works best because of its fiber length. The barbs along the fiber shaft allow the fabric to weave itself together during the wash process. Synthetic and acrylic yarns will not felt properly because they lack these important qualities. Even a small amount of synthetic content will inhibit the felting process, but there are exceptions (see Cesca, page 138). Mohair yarn, which is used in most of the felted styles in this book, is an exception. Mohair felts beautifully, adding tremendous color and dimension, even though most mohair yarn has anywhere from 10 to 15 % nylon or acrylic. To be effective in felting, mohair yarn should have at least 85% mohair content. Read the label of the yarn you intend to felt with. If it doesn't have the qualities for successful felting, set it aside for another project.

Felting a Knitted Hat

Once you've knitted the hat you're going to felt, you'll probably think you did it wrong because the piece will be so large it will look as though it's meant to be worn by a giant. Don't worry—the hat needs room to shrink to create the tight fabric that's characteristic of a felted hat. Before you get ready to wash the hat, sew in the loose yarn ends and closely follow the felting directions.

PREPARING THE HAT FOR FELTING

Check to make sure you have sewn in any yarn ends that might have been left hanging on the hat; if you sew them in before felting, they get woven into the hat with the felting process and the result looks more professional.

Place the knitted hat in a pillowcase (this prevents the fibers from coming loose in your machine) and zip it shut or close it with a heavy-duty elastic or rubber band. (Note: I use pillowcase covers because they zip closed quickly, but I sometimes find that the zippers don't stay zipped and the hat falls out). You can felt more than one hat at a time, but each should be in its own pillowcase so the fibers don't mix and the hats don't discolor each other.

A word on "adding a sneaker": Felting instructions in books often suggest adding a sneaker to the wash to increase agitation and friction. Quite honestly, I have tried felting with and without sneakers many times and don't see that it makes much difference, at least with the hat styles included in this book. This is probably because mohair, with its fabulous luster and long-length fiber, is used in all but one felted pattern.

FELTING THE HAT

When it comes to felting, each washing machine has its own personality and will felt differently. This is due to a number of factors, including the size of the barrel of the machine, whether it's a top or side-load, the mineral nature of the water, how hot the water gets, and the length of each cycle. These factors aren't standardized across machine brands. However, with a little bit of finessing, there are ways to overcome these uncertainties, allowing you to be the fiber artist you want to be.

If you can't control a machine's behavior, the temperature of the hot water, or the water's mineral content, you can control other factors that will bring you success.

■ Use a top-loading machine (front-loading machines may not soak the hat long enough).

■ Carefully consider the number of wash cycles to use (one may not be enough). Check your felted items after each cycle to see whether they have to be felted further by going through another cycle. Don't automatically run them through again without checking between cycles.

Note: You'll need to add a small amount of detergent to the machine before running a cycle.

■ After the first cycle, take the elastic off the pillowcase or unzip the cover to examine your piece. It will horrify you at first to see the clump of material in your hand, but have no fear—the magic happens in the forming.

■ Try the hat on between cycles. If it's too small, keep stretching it. If it's too large, toss it in the washer again. However, before you begin the wash process, take a moment to read and study the photos on Shaping and Forming the Felted Hat (see page 21), because this is what you will have to do immediately after the wash cycle has been completed.

SHAPING AND FORMING THE FELTED HAT

Take the piece out of the pillowcase and form as follows.

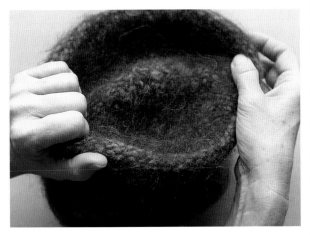

SHAPE THE CROWN

Hold the hat with two hands and pull it in opposite directions. Turn the hat 90 degrees, and stretch out the crown again.

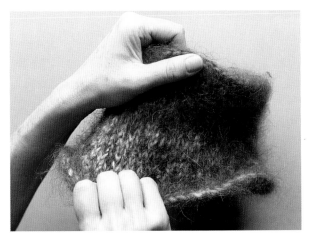

SHAPE THE SIDES

With one hand, hold the rim of the crown and with the other hand pull the hat down. Continue this around the entire hat, taking special care to pull out the bottom rim of the hat.

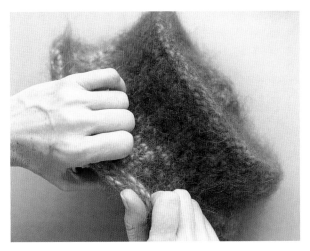

SHAPE THE BRIM

The brim of the hat might have curled upward in the wash. To unfold it, use your fingers and thumbs and pry it loose all the way around.

FIT THE HAT

If possible, try the hat on the person who will be wearing it. If it seems too tight, skip to the next step. If it's way too large, you'll want to toss it in the machine again for another go-round; but this time don't use detergent and run it on a shorter cycle.

DRYING THE HAT

Place the hat on a hat form, or use an upturned cooking pot, and continue pulling out the hat to get the shape you desire. A hat form allows you to balance the size with your head and body while shaping and pulling out the hat, but it's not necessary. See Yarn and Supply Sources on page 144 for information about plastic hat form vendors. The hat will need to dry for at least a day or two. You can put it near a heater to speed the process, but it will still take a few days because of the denseness of the weave.

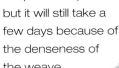

FINISHING TOUCHES

Now comes the really fun part—making the hat design uniquely your own by adding embellishments. There are endless ways to do so. Use the basic shape and color palette of the hat to inspire your choice of decorative elements.

Consider a wide range of embellishment. Well-placed or interesting buttons can add a lot of zip to many hats patterns. Old silver charms strategically placed could add interest as well. Antique pins in silver or Bakelite are attractive and convenient because they can be easily removed for washing and changed to suit a look. Search flea markets or online auctions for the perfect accent piece that adds a bit if dash to your design.

Embroidery or crewelwork on a brim is charming and it doesn't have to be extensive to make an impact—a stitched design off to the side at the front will do just the trick. Easier still, use the blanket stitch (see page 28) in a contrasting color on the edge of the brim—traditional, yet always attractive.

KNITTING BEADS INTO A HAT

It's very easy to create fanciful looks with beads and sequins (take a look at the Damien hat below). Before you begin to knit your hat, string the total amount of beads or sequins you'll need onto the skein of yarn you'll be using. Make sure that the bead or sequin hole will take two widths of the yarn, as you'll be using a darning needle to sew on the beads. As you work the hat, you'll have to keep pushing the beads back until the point where you begin to knit the beads into the hat, which is done as follows.

KNITTING ON THE FIRST BEAD

Pull a bead/sequin close up to where you will make your next stitch.

PUSHING THE BEAD THROUGH THE STITCH

Knit the stitch, pushing the bead/sequin toward the front and through the stitch.

SECURING THE BEAD

In the next rnd, when you are knitting the stitch with a bead on it, knit into the back of the loop on the left hand side of the needle, keeping the bead/sequin to the front.

KNITTED APPLIQUÉS

You can knit just about anything and sew in onto a hat. It doesn't necessarily have to be something identifiable like a flower—it could just be a design element like a circle or square. If you'd like to experiment, try knitting a classic rose using the following instructions.

ROSE

MATERIALS

- 2 strands of worsted weight yarn, preferably in two different shades of pink, coral, or red

- 5.25mm (size 9 U.S.) dpn

- Darning needle

With two strands of yarn held together, CO 38 sts.

k 1 row.

p 1 row.

k1, m1, repeat around—57 sts.

p 1 row.

k 1 row.

p 1 row.

k 1 row.

p 1 row.

BO, leaving a 15"/38cm end of wool.

STARTING THE COIL

SHAPING THE ROSE

Thread the darning needle and begin to coil the piece, first creating the center, basting it on the back as you coil.

Attach the finished rose to the hat.

Thread a darning needle onto this end and coil the piece round and round, basting the coil together as you go.

Handmade felted appliqués harmonize wonderfully with felted hats. There are two basic ways to make them: you can knit and felt a flat piece of material and then cut out the appliqué, or you can knit and felt individual appliqués that have already been shaped in the knitting. The method you choose will determine the finished appearance of the piece. Appliqués cut from a felted fabric will have a rougher, more country, painterly look around the edges, whereas the individually knitted appliqués with be somewhat more refined. Try both and see what you prefer. Making appliqués is a great way to use up those bags of wool scraps hiding out in the closet.

METHOD II:
KNITTING INDIVIDUAL FELTED APPLIQUÉS

DAISY

MATERIALS NEEDED

- Scraps of mohair and chunky-weight wool yarn
- Knitting needles: 6.5 mm (size 10½ U.S.) dpn
- Darning needle
- Sharp scissors

With dpn and holding two strands of yarn together, CO 12 sts and divide among 3 dpn or do the Wrap Method described on page 14.

Rnd 1 and all odd rnds: K.

Rnd 2: *k1, m1,* repeat around—18 sts.

Rnd 4: *k2, m1,* repeat around—24 sts.

Repeat rnds 1 and 2, each adding an additional k st before each m1 until there are 4 k sts before each m1— 36 sts total.

K 1 rnd.

BO.

FINISHING

Using a darning needle, sew in yarn ends.

The finished piece is in the shape of a circle. Make all the appliqués you need and felt the batch together following the instructions on pages 20 and 21. After they've been felted, stretch and pull the pieces, laying them flat on a towel to dry.

METHOD I:
CREATING A FLAT PIECE OF FELTED MATERIAL

This is the fastest and easiest method for making the widest variety of forms. Just keep in mind that your initial fabric size will shrink 10 to 20% once felted.

Follow the same process used for the felted hats in this collection. Use a size 5.50 or 6.50mm (size #10 or #10 ½ U.S.) needle and two strands of yarn, one mohair and the other wool. Cast on the number of stitches you'll need to make a square of fabric. For example, a 10 x 10-inch (24 x 24 cm) piece of fabric will require about 35 sts. Knit the stitches in a simple stockingnette stitch (alternately k 1 row, p 1 row) for however long or as much as you think you will need for the appliqué you have in mind. When your piece is as long as you want it, follow the felting instructions on pages 20 and 21. Once the felted fabric dries, you can cut out any shape that you want and apply it to the hat.

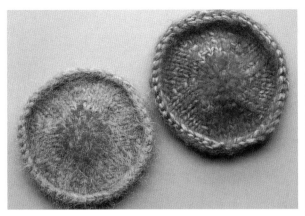

FORMING A DAISY

Start with a knitted, felted circle.

TRIMMING THE EDGES

Trim off the cast-off edge.

CREATING PETALS

Make cuts into the circle at four equidistant positions around the edge. Think of it as making cuts at 12:00, 3:00, 6:00, and 9:00 o'clock on a watch. Don't cut all the way to the middle as you will need a center for attaching the flower to the hat. Make four additional cuts between the cuts you have already made, which will give you a total of eight petals.

SHAPING THE DAISY

To define the petal shape, cut a slice from each petal all the way around.

ATTATCHING THE DAISY

Slip the hat on to see where to place an appliqué. If only one flower is used, attach it to the hat, off to the side. However, if there are three flowers, place one directly in front and the two others, on each side of it. Tack the appliqué down using either common or safety pins. For the center of the flower, thread a darning needle with yarn and make French knots (see page 28) until the entire center is filled. If you don't know how to embroider, cut out a piece of felt the size of the center and tack the felt center down using simple basting stitches.

PEONY

MATERIALS

- 1 strand of mohair yarn

- 1 strand chunky 100% wool yarn, preferably in two different shades of pink, coral, or red 6.50mm (size 10 ½ U.S.) dpn

- Darning needle

With dpn, CO 24 sts.

k 1 row.

p 1 row.

*k1, m1,*repeat around—36 sts.

p 1 rnd.

k 1 rnd.

Repeat last two rounds.

p 1 rnd.

BO, leaving a 15˝/38cm end of wool.

Follow the felting instructions on pages 20 and 21 to felt the appliqué.

SHAPING THE PEONY

Thread the darning needle and begin to coil the piece, first creating the center by folding over the outer edge. Baste back into the coiled piece as you go around.

ATTACHING THE PEONY

With a darning needle and matching yarn, attach the finished peony to the hat.

SUNFLOWER

MATERIALS

- Scraps of mohair and chunky weight wool yarn

- Sharp scissors

- 6.50mm (size 10 ½ U.S.) dpn

- Darning needle

With dpn and two strands of yarn together, CO 12 sts and divide among 3 needles or do the Wrap Method described on page 14.

Rnd 1 and all odd rnds: K.

Rnd 2: *k1, m1,* repeat around—18 st.

Rnd 4: * k2, m1,* repeat around—24 st.

Repeat rnds 1 and 2, each time adding an additional k st before each m1 until there are 4 k sts before each m1—36 sts total.

K 8 rnds.

BO.

FINISHING

Using a darning needle, sew in yarn ends.

When the piece is complete, it should be in the shape of a circle with rolled edges. Make all the appliqués you need and felt them in a batch together following the instructions on pages 20 and 21. After washing the pieces, stretch and pull them, laying them flat on a towel to dry.

SHAPING THE SUNFLOWER

Using a pair of sharp, heavy-duty scissors, remove the curled edging.

CREATING PETALS

With the scissors, remove triangle shapes from the edge of the felted piece up to the rim where it starts to bend over into the center. Continue cutting these triangle shapes around the edge.

Slip the hat on first to see where to place the appliqué. Pin the appliqué in place. Using a darning needle threaded with yarn, attach it to the hat with French knots, making enough knots to cover the entire middle of the flower.

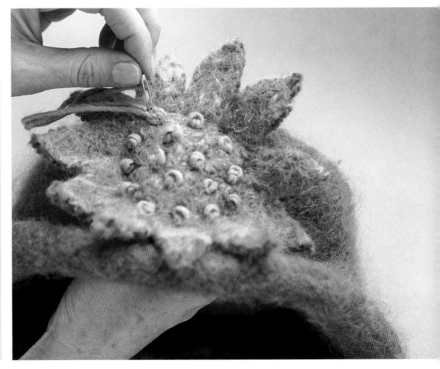

EMBROIDERED EMBELLISHMENTS

A few stitches here and there (especially when created in contrasting colors) can create an entirely new look on any hat. For the felted style Clem (page 136), the brim was blanket-stitched around the upturned edge, then a few flowers were added in the lazy daisy stitch, topped off with a some French knots to make the colors really pop.

Even if you've never embroidered before, it's easy to master these common stitches. Experiment with different color combinations and yarn types to add your own flair to these time-tested designs.

■ Blanket Stitch

Working from the left to right, bring the needle out to your edge. Make an upright stitch to the right with the needle pointed down. Catch the thread under the point of the needle as you come out on the edge.

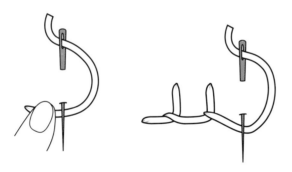

■ French Knot

Starting on the right side of your work, wrap the thread twice around the point of your needle, pull it tight, and insert the needle next to where it came out. Hold the thread taut to form a knot and pull the needle through the wrong side of the fabric to secure it.

■ Lazy Daisy Stitch

Bring the needle to the right side of the material. Hold down the thread with your thumb so that a loop will form. Insert the needle at the spot where the thread emerged. Bring it up a short distance from this point. When the thread is drawn through, reinsert the needle, making a small stitch over the end of the loop to hold the loop stitch in place.

OTHER EMBELLISHMENTS

MAKING POMPOMS

To start off, you'll need something stiff to wrap yarn around, such as a piece of cardboard with a hole in its center. (You can even use three fingers held together if nothing else is handy). The board should be as wide as the pompom that you wish to make. **(a)** Wrap the yarn around 15 to 20 times, fewer times if you want it to be floppy, more times if you want it to be firmly packed. **(b)** Tie a thread tightly around the middle, then cut the ends open and trim. **(c)** Fluff the ends of the yarn into a circle. **(d)** Remove the cardboard from the center.

a

TASSELS

A tassel begins the same way a pompom does—by wrapping yarn around a stiff board (or your fingers!) the length of what you would like the finished tassel to be. Remember, the tassel can always be trimmed, but it can't grow. **(a)** To neatly secure the bundle of thread, take a separate thread about 24″/61cm long, and create a loop vertical to the thread bundle with the string hanging down. Wrap the thread around the top of the bundle about 6 to 8 times. **(b)** Insert the thread through the loop and pull on the thread below to drag the loose thread end into the wrapped top threads to secure it in place. Snip the ends and attach it to the hat.

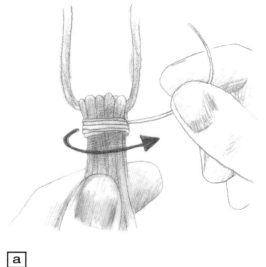

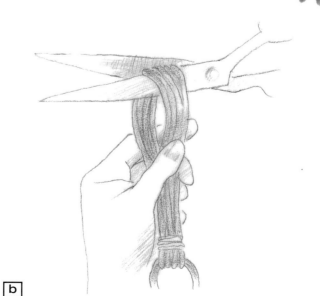

PICKING A HAT STYLE

The style of hat you choose will no doubt depend on your own taste, but rest assured, there's something for everyone in this collection. Here are some ideas to think about when deciding which style to make.

HAT STYLE AND SHAPE

Faces, like works of art, look different in different frames. You might already know what style looks good and feels comfortable on you, but if you don't, I encourage you to experiment and play dressup in stores that carry hats. Don't be afraid to try on a style you can't imagine wearing—it might look fabulous! As a rule, hats with brims, commonly referred to as bucket hats, are kind to most face shapes. A brim adds extra framing and softens the face. Brimless hats (sometimes referred to as pillbox styles) and caps put your face more out in front, in the spotlight. The pillbox is not a universally flattering style, but if you have the panache, and perhaps a silk or challis scarf wrapped around your neck, you can pull it off. Here are some combinations of styles and head features to consider.

The shape of a hat crown often conveys the hat's level of formality. For example, a knitted cap with a rounded crown tends to look sporty and informal, whereas a pillbox or bucket hat tends to look more formal. These are just basic guidelines, though. Adding embellishments can make a sporty hat look more formal or a dressy one more playful.

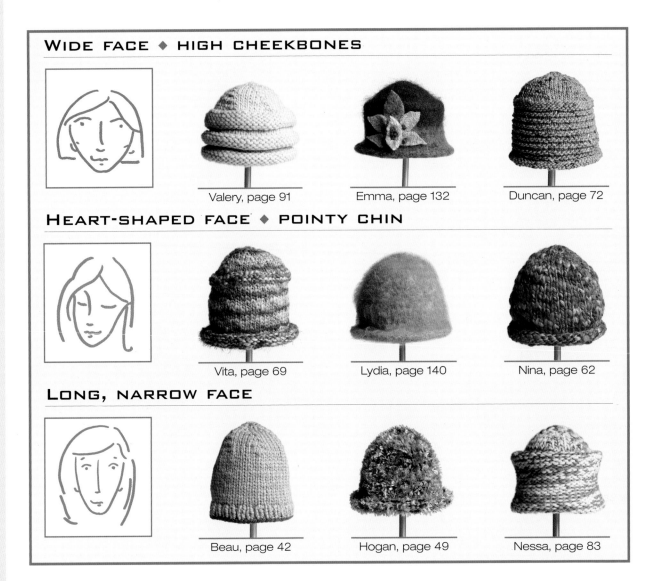

WIDE FACE ◆ HIGH CHEEKBONES

Valery, page 91

Emma, page 132

Duncan, page 72

HEART-SHAPED FACE ◆ POINTY CHIN

Vita, page 69

Lydia, page 140

Nina, page 62

LONG, NARROW FACE

Beau, page 42

Hogan, page 49

Nessa, page 83

SIZING AND FIT

Heads come in different sizes! The idea of one-size-fits-all just doesn't apply when it comes to hats. If you measure the head circumferences of family members and friends, you'll find a range of sizes. To ensure a proper fit, it's important to determine the head circumference of the person for whom you'll be knitting. Once you know the size, you'll need to consider the fit—how the hat sits on the head. Each hat style fits differently. For example, Skip (see page 52), inspired by the traditional seaman's cap, should fit snuggly on the head. Its wide-ribbed brim will ensure that it will not come off in windy or inclement weather. On the other hand, Violet Seed (see page 88) and other pillbox shapes look better when floating down over your head. Berets are versatile. They can be worn off to the side or pulled to the back. As a rule of thumb, tighter fitting hats tend to look sportier, whereas hats that rest more loosely on the head appear more formal. To accommodate a wide range of sizes and allow for a variety of "fits," the patterns in the book specify two sizes, which should fit most adults.

Head circumference

Medium	20 to 21"/51 to 53cm
Large	22 to 23"/56 to 58cm

COLOR

There's a good chance you already know which colors complement your looks and complexion, but here are some tips in case you need guidance.

Lighter colors soften the face, whereas darker and more intense colors create contrast and can appear harsh, depending on your skin tone. I love yarn shops that provide mirrors so that you can hold up the yarn to your face and see how it works with your skin tone. The perennial favorite hat color is black, and although very chic, it can appear too harsh. Most likely you will want your hat to "go with" or harmonize with the coat or jacket you intend to wear with it. However, that doesn't necessarily mean you want to match it hue for hue, either: Mix it up and be daring.

TIPS ON WEARING KNITTED OR FELTED HATS

Nobody likes a squished brow. Wear your hat a bit loosely—you'll feel more comfortable, and depending on the hat, it might look more elegant. However, you'll want a cap to be snug for protection against inclement weather.

If you're accustomed to wearing a knit hat and a scarf at the same time, try using a scarf that is not knitted, such as wool challis or silk, for added contrast and interest.

When you first buy or make a hat, practice trying it on with a mirror and then without. Take some time to play with your look—try tilting the hat different ways until you find what fits right and looks right on you. Remember what you did to create that look so the next time you can do it spontaneously as you're rushing out the door.

Develop a hat wardrobe so that you have a special look for each style of jacket, coat, or sweater in your closet.

HAT VOCABULARY

Before you begin to knit, take a look at the diagram below, which defines the parts of a hat as they'll be referred to in the patterns. Undoubtedly, you will want to come back to this page just to make sure you're headed (no pun intended!) in the right direction.

a Top of Crown

b Crown

c Turn of Crown (flat-tops have them, round tops don't)

d Rise

e Brim

f Circumference

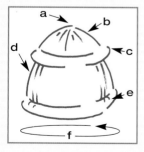

CAPS

IS THE CAP. TRADITIONALLY, IT'S BEEN KNOWN FOR ITS WARMTH, RATHER THAN ITS STYLE, BUT THIS COLLECTION PROVES THAT THE TWO IDEAS AREN'T MUTUALLY EXCLUSIVE. TRY KNITTING A SIMPLE, TIME-HONORED DESIGN WITH A CONTEMPORARY COLOR PALETTE. ADD A NEW TWIST, LIKE A WIDE BRIM, OR A FUN-FUR FRINGE AROUND THE EDGE. OR CHALLENGE YOURSELF BY CREATING A DELICATE LACE-LIKE TEXTURE AND A ROLLED BRIM. THERE ARE ENDLESS WAYS TO INTERPRET THIS FAMILIAR FORM AND MAKE IT YOUR OWN.

SKILL LEVEL

Easy

SIZE

Medium
20 to 21"/51 to 53cm

Large
22 to 23"/56 to 58cm

HERE'S A HEAD-HUGGING CAP

FOR THE FLAPPER, RAPPER, OR PREPPY IN YOU! KNIT IT IN WOOL, AND YOU'VE GOT A CASUAL ACCESSORY; KNIT IT IN METALLIC OR SILK YARN (WITH BEADS!), AND IT'S JUST RIGHT FOR A NIGHT ON THE TOWN.

CHUNKY WEIGHT
JESSE IN TURQUOISE
AND CLEMATIS

MATERIALS

- Color A: Approx 45(55)yd/41(50)m chunky weight yarn
- Color B: Approx 55(45)yd/50(41)m chunky weight yarn
- 5.75mm (size 10 U.S.) dpn and 16"/41cm cn *or size to obtain gauge*
- Stitch marker
- Darning needle

GAUGE

12 sts = 4"/10cm

Always check gauge.

CROWN

Using dpn and A, CO 12 sts and divide among 3 dpn, *or* do the Wrap Method described on page 14.

Rnd 1 and all odd rnds: K.

Rnd 2: *k1, m1,* repeat around—18 sts total.

Rnd 4: *k2, m1,* repeat around—24 sts total.

Rnd 6: *k3, m1,* repeat around—30 sts total.

Repeat rnds 1 and 2, each time adding an additional k st before each m1, until there are 8(9) sts before each m1—60(66) sts total.

Switch to cn.

K 1 rnd.

RISE

With B, k for 6½(7)"/17(18)cm from top of crown.

BRIM

Using color A, k 1 rnd.

K1/p1 rib for 3 rnds.

BO loosely in k1/p1 rib.

FINISHING

Sew in all ends.

This hat was knit with: Classic Elite's *Two.Two,* 100% wool, 1¾oz/50g = 55yd/50m

Large (on model)

Color A: 1 ball, color #1585 (pumpkin)

Color B: 1 ball, color #1532 (zinnia)

Medium

Color A: 1 ball, color #1504 (turquoise)

Color B: 1 ball, color #1592 (clematis)

VARIATION

Use bulky weight yarn for a more substantial look and greater warmth.

MATERIALS

- Color A: Approx 65(75)yd/59(69)m bulky weight yarn
- Color B: Approx 75(65)yd/69(59)m bulky weight yarn
- 8mm (size 11 U.S.) dpn and 16"/41cm cn *or size to obtain gauge*
- Stitch marker
- Darning needle

GAUGE

10 sts = 4"/10cm

Always check gauge.

CROWN

Using dpn and A, CO 12 sts and divide among 3 dpn, *or* do the Wrap Method described on page 14.

**BULKY WEIGHT
JESSE IN OATMEAL
AND PINE**

**BULKY WEIGHT
JESSE IN OATMEAL
AND SABLE**

Rnd 1 and all odd rnds: K.

Rnd 2: *k1, m1,* repeat around—
18 sts total.

Rnd 4: *k2, m1,* repeat around—
24 sts total.

Rnd 6: *k3, m1,* repeat around—
30 sts total.

Repeat rnds 1 and 2, each time adding
an additional k st before each m1, until
there are 6(7) sts before each m1—
48(54) sts total.

Switch to cn.

K 1 rnd.

RISE

With B, k for $6^{1}/_{2}(7)$"/17(18)cm from
top of crown.

BRIM

Using color A, k 1 rnd.

K1/p1 rib for 2 rnds.

BO loosely in k1/p1 rib.

FINISHING

Sew in all ends.

This hat was knit with: Brown Sheep's
Burley Spun, 100% wool, 8oz/226g =
132yd/121m

Medium

Color A: 1 ball, color #BS115 (oatmeal)

Color B: 1 ball, color #BS07 (sable)

Large

Color A: 1 ball, color #BS115 (oatmeal)

Color B: 1 ball, color #BS120 (pine)

SKILL LEVEL

Easy

SIZE

Medium
20 to 21"/51 to 53cm

Large
22 to 23"/56 to 58cm

THE TEXTURE AND COLOR CONTRASTS

BETWEEN THE CROWN AND THE WIDE, UPTURNED RIBBED BRIM MAKE THIS HAT SPECIAL. WHEN CHOOSING YARN FOR THE CROWN, THINK FLUFFY AND TEXTURED, WHEREAS THE RIBBED BRIM SHOULD BE DONE IN NON-TEXTURED, OR PLAIN WORSTED AND SPORT WEIGHT YARNS.

MATERIALS

- Color A: Approx 80(90)yd/73(82)m bulky weight yarn
- Color B: Approx 40(45)yd/37(41)m bulky weight yarn
- 8mm (size 11 U.S.) dpn and 16"/41cm and 24"/61cm cn *or size to obtain gauge*
- Stitch marker
- Darning needle

GAUGE

8 sts = 4"/10cm

Always check gauge.

CROWN

Using dpn and A, CO 12 sts and divide among 3 dpn, *or* do the Wrap Method described on page 14.

Rnd 1 and all odd rnds: K.

Rnd 2: *k1, m1,* repeat around— 18 sts total.

Rnd 4: *k2, m1,* repeat around— 24 sts total.

Rnd 6: *k3, m1,* repeat around— 30 sts total.

Repeat rnds 1 and 2, each time adding an additional k st before each m1, until there are 5(6) k sts before each m1— 42(48) sts total.

Switch to cn; pm to denote beg/end of rnd (16˝/41cm for *Medium,* 24˝/61cm for *Large*) K for 7˝/18cm from top of crown.

RIBBED BRIM

With B, k 1 rnd.

K1/p1 rib for 5½"/14cm or until piece measures 12½"/32cm from the top of crown.

BO loosely in k1/p1 rib.

**BULKY WEIGHT
PAT IN RED
AND ORANGE**

FINISHING

Sew in ends.

This hat was knit with: Blue Sky Alpacas' *Bulky Alpaca,* 50% alpaca/50% wool, 3½oz/100g = 45yd/41m

Medium (on model)

Color A: 1 ball, color #1015 (orange)

Color B: 1 ball, color #1016 (gold)

Large

Color A: 1 ball, color #1010 (red)

Color B: 1 ball, color #1015 (orange)

VARIATION

Chunky weight yarn gives you a different texture.

MATERIALS

- Color A: Approx 120(130)yd/110(119)m chunky weight yarn

- Color B: Approx 60(70)yd/55(64)m chunky weight yarn

- 6.50mm (size 10½ U.S.) dpn and 16"/41cm and 24"/61cm cn *or size to obtain gauge*

- Stitch marker

- Darning needle

GAUGE

12 sts = 4"/10cm

Always check gauge.

CROWN

Using dpn and A, CO 12 sts and divide among 3 dpn, *or* do the Wrap Method described on page 14.

Rnd 1 and all odd rnds: K.

Rnd 2: *k1, m1,* repeat around—18 sts total.

Rnd 4: *k2, m1,* repeat around—24 sts total.

Rnd 6: *k3, m1,* repeat around—30 sts total.

Repeat rnds 1 and 2, each time adding an additional k st before each m1, until there are 8(9) k sts before each m1—60(66) sts total.

Switch to cn; pm to denote beg/end of rnd (16"/41cm for *Medium,* 24"/61cm for *Large*) K for 7"/18cm from top of crown.

RIBBED BRIM

With B, k 1 rnd.

K1/p1 rib for 5½"/14cm or until piece measures 12½"/32cm from the top of crown.

BO loosely in k1/p1 rib.

FINISHING

Sew in ends.

This hat was knit with: Brown Sheep's *Lamb's Pride Bulky,* 85% wool/15% mohair, 4oz/113g = 125yd/114m

Medium

Color A: 1 ball, color #M-97 (rust)

Color B: 1 ball, color #M-110 (orange you glad)

Large

Color A: 1 ball, color #M-83 (raspberry)

Color B: 1 ball, color #M-81 (barn red)

CHUNKY WEIGHT PAT IN RASPBERRY AND BARN RED

CHUNKY WEIGHT PAT IN RUST AND ORANGE YOU GLAD

BEAU

SKILL LEVEL

Easy

SIZE

Medium
20 to 21"/51 to 53cm

Large
22 to 23"/56 to 58cm

HERE'S A CLOCHE-STYLE HAT

THAT EASILY ROLLS UP IN YOUR COAT POCKET. THE SLIGHTLY FLARED, RIBBED RIM—EDGED WITH A SINGLE CONTRASTING COLOR—MAKES THIS ONE A CHARMER. THE HAT IS MEANT TO JUST LIGHTLY HUG THE HEAD. COMBINING TWO DIFFERENT COLORED STRANDS RESULTS IN THE HEAVIER WEIGHT SPECIFIED. IF YOU CHOOSE A CONTRASTING TRIM AT THE EDGE OF THE BRIM, MAKE SURE IT'S THE SAME WEIGHT AS THE BODY OF THE HAT.

MATERIALS

- Color A: Approx 90yd(92)/82(84)m chunky weight yarn
- Color B: Approx 8yd/7m bulky weight yarn
- 6mm (size 10½ U.S.) dpn and 24"/61cm cn *or size to obtain gauge*
- Stitch marker
- Darning needle

GAUGE

12 sts = 4"/10cm

Always check gauge.

CROWN

Using dpn and A, CO 12 sts and divide among 3 dpn, or do the Wrap Method described on page 14.

Rnd 1 and all odd rnds: K.

Rnd 2: *k1, m1,* repeat around—18 sts total.

Rnd 4: *k2, m1,* repeat around—24 sts total.

Rnd 6: *k3, m1,* repeat around—30 sts total.

Repeat rnds 1 and 2, each time adding an additional k st before each m1, until there are 8 (9) k sts before each m1—60(66) sts total.

K1 rnd.

Switch to cn; pm to denote beg/end.

RISE

K from the top of crown for 6½(7)"/17(18)cm.

BRIM

K2, m1, repeat around. K1/p1, rib for 4 rnds.

Switch to B.

BO loosely in k1/p1 rib.

FINISHING

Sew in all ends.

This hat was knit with: Classic Elite's *Gatsby,* 70% wool/15% viscose/15% nylon, 3½oz/100g = 90yd/84m

Medium (on model)

Color A: 1 ball, color #2113 (black)

Color B: 1 ball, color #2132 (raspberry)

Large (on background model)

Color A: 1 ball, color #2103 (heather grey)

Color B: 1 ball, color #2132 (raspberry)

Variation

A different combination of yarns creates interesting results.

Materials

- Color A: Approx 90(100)yd/82(91)m bulky weight yarn
- Color B: Approx 8yd/7m bulky weight yarn
- 7mm (size 11 U.S.) dpn and 24"/61cm cn *or size to obtain gauge*
- Stitch marker
- Darning needle

Gauge

10 sts = 4"/10cm

Always check gauge.

Crown

Using dpn and A, CO 12 sts and divide among 3 dpn, or do the Wrap Method described on page 14.

Rnd 1 and all odd rnds: K.

Rnd 2: *k1, m1,* repeat around—
18 sts total.

Rnd 4: *k2, m1,* repeat around—
24 sts total.

Rnd 6: *k3, m1,* repeat around—
30 sts total.

Repeat rnds 1 and 2, each time adding an additional k st before each m1, until there are 6 (7) k sts before each m1—48(54) sts total.

K1 rnd.

Switch to cn; pm to denote beg/end.

Rise

K from the top of crown for 7¹/₂(7¹/₂)"/18(18)cm.

Brim

K2, m1, repeat around. K1/p1, rib for 3 rnds.

Switch to B.

BO loosely in k1/p1 rib.

Finishing

Sew in all ends.

This hat was knit with: Takhi Stacy Charles' *Baby,* 100% wool, 3¹/₂oz/100g = 60yd/54m

Large

Color A: 2 balls, color #41 (hot multi)

Color B: 8yd/7m, color #22 (dark olive)

Medium

Color A: 2 balls, color #39 (light aqua)

Color B: 8yd/7m, color #314 (light olive)

BULKY WEIGHT BEAU
IN HOT MULTI
AND DARK OLIVE

BULKY WEIGHT BEAU
IN LIGHT AQUA AND
LIGHT OLIVE

SKILL LEVEL

Beginner

SIZE

Medium
20 to 21"/51 to 53cm

Large
22 to 23"/56 to 58cm

THE WIDE, UPTURNED BRIM

OF THIS HAT MAKES A STRONG STYLE STATEMENT. THE COMPLETED PIECE WILL APPEAR SOMEWHAT WIDER THAN YOU MIGHT EXPECT AT THE BOTTOM EDGE. THAT'S SO YOU CAN FOLD THE HAT BACK ONTO ITSELF TO CREATE THE HIGH, WIDE BRIM.

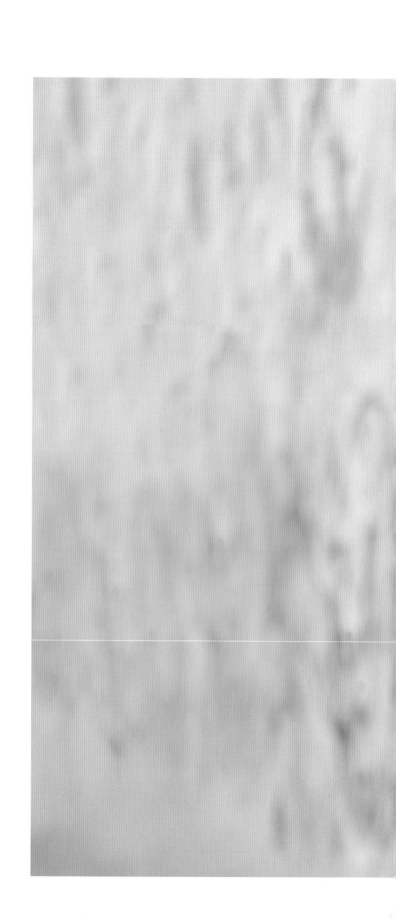

MATERIALS

- Approx 140(150)yd/128(137)m bulky weight yarn
- 8mm (size 11 U.S.) dpn and 24"/61cm cn *or size to obtain gauge*
- Stitch marker
- Darning needle

GAUGE

10 sts = 4"/10cm

Always check gauge.

CROWN

Using dpn, CO 12 sts and divide among 3 dpn, *or* do the Wrap Method described on page 14.

Rnd 1 and all odd rnds: K.

Rnd 2: *k1, m1,* repeat around—18 sts total.

Rnd 4: *k2, m1,* repeat around—24 sts total.

Rnd 6: *k3, m1,* repeat around—30 sts total.

Repeat rnds 1 and 2, each time adding an additonal k st before each m1 st, until there are 6(7) k sts before each m1 st—48(54) sts total.

Switch to cn; pm to denote beg/end of the rnd.

K 1 rnd.

RISE AND BRIM

K 13"/33cm from top of crown.

BO loosely by knitting.

FINISHING

Sew in all ends.

Fold back the brim until it almost reaches the crown. It should stay in place, but it can also be tacked down in several places at the top to prevent slippage.

> This hat was knit with: Classic Elite's *Tigress,* 100% wool, 7oz/200g = 181yd/165 m
>
> *Medium* (on model)
> 1 ball, color #7076 (sophisticat)

VARIATION

A solid bulky weight yarn creates a versatile look.

MATERIALS

- Approx 110(120)yd/101(110)m bulky weight yarn
- 9mm (size 13 U.S.) dpn and 24"/61cm cn *or size to obtain gauge*
- Stitch marker
- Darning needle

GAUGE

8 sts = 4"/10cm

Always check gauge.

BULKY WEIGHT
BETTE IN TEAL

CROWN

Using dpn, CO 12 sts and divide among 3 dpn, or do the Wrap Method described on page 14.

Rnd 1 and all odd rnds: K.

Rnd 2: *k1, m1,* repeat around—18 sts total.

Rnd 4: *k2, m1,* repeat around—24 sts total.

Rnd 6: *k3, m1,* repeat around—30 sts total.

Repeat rnds 1 and 2, each time adding an additonal k st before each m1 st, until there are 5(6) k sts before each m1 st—42(48) sts total.

Switch to cn; pm to denote beg/end of the rnd.

K 1 rnd.

RISE AND BRIM

K 13"/33cm from top of crown.

BO loosely by knitting.

FINISHING

Sew in all ends.

Fold back the brim until it almost reaches the crown. It should stay in place, but it can also be tacked down in several places at the top to prevent slippage.

> This hat was knit with: Blue Sky Alpacas' *Bulky Alpaca,* 50% alpaca/50% wool, 3oz/100g = 45yd/41m
>
> *Large*
> 3 balls, color #1011 (teal)

HOGAN

SKILL LEVEL

Easy

SIZE

Medium
20 to 21"/51 to 53cm

Large
22 to 23"/56 to 58cm

THIS FUZZY LITTLE BELL CAP

CAN BE ROLLED UP AND STUFFED INTO A POCKET AND STILL LOOK AS GOOD AS NEW WHEN IT'S RETRIEVED. SHIFTING IT ON AN ANGLE CREATES A MORE GLAMOROUS LOOK.

MATERIALS

- Color A: Approx 70(95)yd/64(87)m worsted weight yarn
- Color B: Approx 70(95)yd/64(87)m eyelash yarn
- 6.50mm (size 10½ U.S.) dpn and 16"/41cm and 24"/61cm cn *or size to obtain gauge*
- Stitch marker
- Darning needle

GAUGE

10 sts (with A and B together) = 4"/10 cm

Always check gauge.

CROWN

Using dpn and A and B together, CO 12 sts and divide among 3 dpn, or do the Wrap Method described on page 14.

Rnd 1 and all odd rnds: K.

Rnd 2: *k1, m1,* repeat around— 18 sts total.

Rnd 4: *k2, m1,* repeat around— 24 sts total.

Rnd 6: *k3, m1,* repeat around— 30 sts total.

Repeat rnds 1 and 2, each time adding an additional k st before each m1, until there are 6(7) sts before each m1— 48(54) sts total.

Switch to cn (16"/41cm for *Medium,* 24"/61cm for *Large*); pm to denote beg/end of rnd.

K for 7"/18cm from top of crown.

BRIM

K2, m1, repeat around.

K 4 rnds.

BO loosely in k1/p1 rib.

FINISHING

Sew in all ends

This hat was knit with: Berroco's *Duo,* 98% wool/2% nylon, $1^3/_4$oz/50g = 55yd/50m and Bernat's *Boa,* 100% polyester, $1^3/_4$oz/50g = 71yd/65m

Medium
Color A: 2 balls, *Duo,* color #3222 (plum)
Color B: 1 ball, *Boa,* color #81305 (parrot)

Large (on model)
Color A: 2 balls, *Duo,* color #3201 (naturale)
Color B: 2 balls, *Boa,* color #81044 (swan)

Large
Color A: 2 balls, *Duo,* color #3263 (navy)
Color B: 2 balls, *Boa,* color #81206 (toucan)

or
Color A: 2 balls, *Duo,* color #3260 (Sky)
Color B: 2 balls, *Boa,* color #81420 (love bird)

HOGAN IN
NAVY AND
TOUCAN

HOGAN IN
PLUM AND
PARROT

HOGAN IN
LOVE BIRD AND SKY

VARIATION

Following the same instructions, try making the pattern with metallic sport weight yarn instead.

This hat was knit with: Berroco's *Lavish*, 40% nylon/32% wool/15% polyester/13% acrylic, 1³/₄oz/50g = 55yd/50m and Rowan's *Yorkshire Tweed DK*, 100% wool, 1³/₄oz/50g = 123yd/113m

Medium

Color A: 2 balls, *Lavish*, color #7329 (mars)

Color B: 1 ball, *Yorkshire Tweed DK*, color #344 (scarlet)

Large

Color A: 2 balls, *Lavish*, color #7319 (Versace)

Color B: 1 ball, *Yorkshire Tweed DK*, color #347 (skip)

HOGAN IN
VERSACE
AND SKIP

HOGAN IN
MARS AND
SCARLET

SKILL LEVEL

Easy

SIZE

Medium
20 to 21"/51 to 53cm

Large
22 to 23"/56 to 58cm

NOTHING COULD BE EASIER TO KNIT

THAN THIS RIBBED SKULLCAP.
WHEN DONE IN A SMALL GAUGE,
THE LOOK IS TRADITIONAL. BUT
TAKE IT UP A NOTCH AND USE A
WIDER GAUGE, AND YOU'RE THERE
WITH THE LATEST OF TRENDS.

MATERIALS

- Approx 140(150)yd/128(137)m heavy worsted weight yarn
- 5.75mm (size 10 U.S.) dpn and 16"/41cm cn *or size to obtain gauge*
- Stitch marker
- Darning needle

GAUGE

12 sts = 4"/10cm

Always check gauge.

SKIP

BRIM AND RISE

Using cn for *Large*, dpn for *Medium*, CO 76(84) sts.

Pm to denote beg/end of rnd.

K2/p2, rib for 12″/30cm.

CROWN

Switch to dpn.

Rnd 1: *k2tog, p2,* repeat around—27(30) sts remain.

Rnd 2: *k1, p2,* repeat around.

Rnd 3: *k1, p2tog,* repeat around—18(20) sts remain.

Rnd 4: *k1, p1,* repeat around.

Rnd 5: K2tog around—9(10) sts remain.

Rnd 6: K.

Rnd 7: K2tog around, ending k1—10(11) sts remain

FINISHING

For the remaining stitches, cut the yarn, leaving a 5″/13cm tail, and string the stitches onto this yarn; pull the stitches tight and sew in the end on the WS.

This hat was knit with Classic Elite's *Montera,* 50% llama/50% wool, 3¹⁄₂oz/100g = 127yd/116m

Medium

2 balls, color #3850
(Cape Breton forest)

VARIATION

For a much more substantial look, use bulky weight yarn and a larger needle.

MATERIALS

- Approx 85(90)yd/78(92)m bulky weight yarn
- 9mm (size 13 U.S.) dpn and 16"/41cm cn *or size to obtain gauge*
- Stitch marker
- Darning needle

GAUGE

10 sts = 4"/10cm

Always check gauge.

BRIM AND RISE

Using cn, CO 36(40) sts.

Pm to denote beg/end of rnd.

K2/p2, rib for 12″/30cm.

CROWN

Switch to dpn.

Rnd 1: *k2tog, p2,* repeat around—27(30) sts remain.

Rnd 2: *k1, p2,* repeat around.

Rnd 3: *k1, p2tog,* repeat around—18(20) sts remain.

Rnd 4: *k1, p1,* repeat around.

Rnd 5: K2tog around—9(10) sts remain.

Rnd 6: K.

Rnd 7: K2tog around.

FINISHING

For the remaining stitches, cut the yarn, leaving a 5″/13cm tail, and string the stitches onto this yarn; pull the stitches tight and sew in the end on the WS.

This hat was knit with: Blue Sky Alpacas' *Bulky Hand Dyes,* 50% wool/50% alpaca, 3¹⁄₂oz/100g = 45yd/41m

Medium

2 balls, color #1013 (dark blue)

SKIP IN DARK BLUE

MARI

SKILL LEVEL
Easy

SIZE
Medium
20 to 21"/51 to 53cm
Large
22 to 23"/56 to 58cm

THE "SEEDED" BAND RISE OF THIS CLOCHE

COMPLEMENTS ANY FACE AND LOOKS GREAT WITH CASUAL OR DRESSY COATS. USING A SINGLE COLOR BEST SHOWCASES THE TEXTURE OF THE SEEDED RISE, BUT FOR A CHANGE, YOU COULD KNIT THE BAND A SEPARATE COLOR AND ATTACH A POMPOM, OR PICK ANOTHER TEXTURED STITCH SUCH AS BASKET WEAVE.

MATERIALS

- Color A: Approx 100(110)yd/91(101)m heavy worsted weight yarn
- Color B: Approx 25(30)yd/23(27)m heavy worsted weight yarn
- 5.25mm (size 9 U.S.) dpn and 16"/41cm cn *or size to obtain gauge*
- Stitch marker
- Darning needle

GAUGE

16 sts = 4"/10cm

Always check gauge.

PATTERN STITCH

SEED STITCH

Rnd 1: *k1, p1,* repeat around.

Rnd 2: *p1, k1,* repeat around.

CROWN

Using dpn and A, CO 12 sts and divide among 3 dpn, *or* do the Wrap Method described on page 14.

Rnd 1 and all odd rnds: K.

Rnd 2: *k1, m1,* repeat around—18 sts total.

Rnd 4: *k2, m1,* repeat around—24 sts total.

Rnd 6: *k3, m1,* repeat around—30 sts total.

Repeat rnds 1 and 2 until there are 11(12) sts before each m1—78 (84) sts total.

Switch to cn; pm to denote beg/end of rnd.

K 1 rnd.

RISE

Knit in seed stitch for 7(7 ½)"/18(19)cm from top of crown.

BRIM/BOTTOM EDGE

With B, K1/p1 rib for 3 rnds.

BO loosely in k1/p1 rib.

FINISHING

Sew in all ends.

This hat was knit with: Classic Elite's *Bazic*, 100% wool, 1¾oz/50g = 65yd/59m

Medium (on model)

Color A: 2 balls, color #2961 (carnation)

Color B: 25 yd/23m, color #2958 (barn red)

Large

Color A: 2 balls, color #2902 (wintergreen)

Color B: 25yd/23m, color 2904 (ancient marine)

HEAVY WORSTED MARI
IN WINTERGREEN AND
ANCIENT MARINE

VARIATION

The look of this hat changes completely when you use bulky weight yarn.

MATERIALS

- Approx 75(85)yd/69(78)m bulky weight yarn

- 6.50mm (size 10½ U.S.) dpn and 24"/61cm cn *or size to obtain gauge*

- Stitch marker

- Darning needle

GAUGE

10 sts = 4"/10cm

Always check gauge.

PATTERN STITCH

SEED STITCH

Rnd 1: *k1, p1,* repeat around.

Rnd 2: *p1, k1,* repeat around.

CROWN

Using dpn, CO 12 sts and divide among 3 dpn, *or* do the Wrap Method described on page 14.

Rnd 1 and all odd rnds: K.

Rnd 2: *k1, m1,* repeat around—18 sts total.

Rnd 4: *k2, m1,* repeat around—24 sts total.

Rnd 6: *k3, m1,* repeat around—30 sts total.

Repeat rnds 1 and 2, each time adding a k st before each m1 until there are 6(7) sts before each m1—48(54) sts total.

Switch to cn; pm to denote beg/end of rnd.

K 1 rnd.

RISE

Knit in seed stitch for 7(7½)"/18(19)cm from top of crown.

BRIM/BOTTOM EDGE

K1/p1 rib for 3 rnds.

BO loosely in k1/p1 rib.

FINISHING

Sew in all ends.

This hat was knit with: Tahki Stacy Charles' *Baby,* 100% wool, 3½oz/100g = 60yd/55m

Medium

2 balls, color #7 (medium blue)

Large

2 balls, color #5 (light blue)

BULKY WEIGHT MARI IN MEDIUM BLUE

BULKY WEIGHT MARI IN LIGHT BLUE

CLARA

SKILL LEVEL

Experienced

SIZE

Medium
20 to 21"/51 to 53cm

Large
22 to 23"/56 to 58cm

THE HEAD-HUGGING CLOCHE

WAS THE ACCESSORY OF CHOICE FOR THE SILENT FILM ACTRESS CLARA BOW. THIS VERSION OF THE CLASSIC STYLE FEATURES A LACY OR MESHED CROWN AND A ROLLED BRIM. IT'S ACTUALLY EASIER TO MAKE THAN IT LOOKS—YOU JUST HAVE TO PAY A BIT MORE ATTENTION WHEN MAKING INCREASES FOR THE CROWN. AFTER THEY'RE COMPLETED, IT'S SMOOTH SAILING.

MATERIALS

- Approx 105(109)yd/96(98)m chunky weight yarn
- 5.25mm (size 9 U.S.) dpn and 16"/41cm cn *or size to obtain gauge*
- Stitch marker
- Darning needle

GAUGE

- 12 sts = 4"/10cm

Always check gauge.

CROWN

Using dpn, CO 12 sts and divide among 3 dpn, *or* do the Wrap Method described on page 14.

Rnd 1: K.

Rnd 2: *k1, m1,* repeat around—18 sts total.

Rnd 3: K.

Rnd 4: *k2, m1,* repeat around—24 sts total.

Rnd 5: (k1, *yo, k2tog,* repeat 2x more, k1) repeat 2x more.

Rnd 6: *k3, m1,* repeat around—30 sts total.

Rnd 7: (k1, *yo, k2tog,* repeat 3x more, k1) repeat 2x more.

Rnd 8: *k4, m1,* repeat around—36 sts total.

Rnd 9: (k1, *yo, k2tog,* repeat 4x more, k1) repeat 2x more.

Rnd 10: *k5, m1,* repeat around—42 sts total.

Rnd 11: (k1, *yo, k2tog,* repeat 5x more, k1) repeat 2x more.

Rnd 12: *k6, m1,* repeat around—48 sts total.

Rnd 13: (k1, *yo, k2tog,* repeat 6x more, k1) repeat 2x more.

Rnd 14: *k7, m1,* repeat around—54 sts total.

Rnd 15: (k1, *yo, k2tog,* repeat 7x more, k1) repeat 2x more.

Rnd 16: *k8, m1,* repeat around—60 sts total.

For *Medium,* skp to Rise; for *Large,* continue as follows:

Rnd 17: (k1, *yo, k2tog,* repeat 8x more, k1) repeat 2x more.

Rnd 18: *k9, m1,* repeat around—66 sts total.

RISE

Switch to cn; pm to denote beg/end of rnd.

(K1, *yo, k2tog* repeat 8x(9x) more, k1) repeat 2x more—60(66) sts total.

K 1 rnd.

Repeat last two rnds for 6 3/4(7 1/4)"/17(18)cm from top of crown.

BRIM

K for 2"/5cm.

BO loosely.

FINISHING

Sew in ends.

This hat was knit with: Rowan's *Polar,* 60% wool/30% alpaca/10% acrylic, 3 1/2oz/100g = 109yd/100m

Medium

1 ball, color #650 (smirk)

Large (on model)

1 ball, color #652 (blue)

CLARA IN SMIRK

NONA

SKILL LEVEL

Intermediate

SIZE

Medium
20 to 21"/51 to 53cm

Large
22 to 23"/56 to 58cm

DRESS UP A SIMPLE ROLLED-BRIM HAT

WITH FRINGE THAT FRAMES THE FACE AND ADDS A LITTLE FUN TO EVEN THE DREARIEST WINTER DAY. BRIGHT, CHEERFUL COLORS ARE A NATURAL FOR THIS DESIGN, AND BULKY WEIGHT YARN ENSURES THAT IT'S NOT JUST STYLISH, BUT SERVICEABLY WARM.

MATERIALS

- Color A: Approx 75(85)yd/ 69(78)m bulky weight yarn
- Color B: Approx 25(25)yd/23(23)m eyelash yarn
- 9mm (size 13 U.S.) dpn and 16"/41cm and 24"/61cm cn *or size to obtain gauge*
- Stitch marker
- Darning needle

GAUGE

8 sts = 4"/10cm

Always check gauge.

CROWN

Using dpn and A, CO 12 sts and divide among 3 dpn, *or* do the Wrap Method described on page 14.

Rnd 1 and all odd rnds: K.

Rnd 2: *k1, m1,* repeat around—18 sts total.

Rnd 4: *k2, m1,* repeat around—24 sts total.

Rnd 6: *k3, m1,* repeat around—30 sts total.

Rnd 8: *k4, m1,* repeat around—36 sts total.

Rnd 10: k5, m1, k6(5), m0(1), k5, m1, k5, m1, k5, m1, k6(5), m0(1)—40(42) sts total.

For *Medium,* skp to Rise; For *Large:*

Rnd 12: k20, m1, k20, m1—44 sts total.

Switch to cn (16"/41cm for *Medium,* 24"/61cm for *Large);* pm to denote beg/end of rnd.

RISE

K until hat is 6¼(6¾)"/16(17)cm long.

Attach a strand of B and with A and B together, knit until hat is 7(7½)"/23(24)cm from top of crown.

BRIM

K3, t1 repeat around, ending k1(2).

K 2 rnds.

BO loosely by knitting.

FINISHING

Sew in ends.

This hat was knit with: Blue Sky Alpacas' *Bulky Alpaca,* 50% alpaca/50% wool, 3½oz/100g = 45yd/41m and Berocco's *Zap,* 100% polyester, 1¾oz/50g = 50yd/46m

Medium

Color A: 2 balls, *Bulky Alpaca,* color #1014 (purple)

Color B: 1 ball, *Zap,* color #3501 (cream)

Large (on model)

Color A: 2 balls, *Bulky Alpaca,* color #1071 (granny smith)

Color B: 2 balls, *Zap,* color #3452 (evolution)

NONA IN PURPLE AND CREAM

NINA

THIS STYLE IS VERY MUCH LIKE THE NONA

(SEE PAGE 60) WITH ONE EXCEPTION: IT CLINGS TO THE HEAD, WHEREAS THE NONA HAS A FLARED BRIM. THIS SIMPLE CAP IS IDEAL FOR USING INTERESTING YARNS WITH LOADS OF TEXTURE AND COLOR. YOUR CHOICE OF TRIM CAN CHANGE THE LOOK DRAMATICALLY. WHEN YOU USE BULKY WEIGHT YARN, IT'S THE WARMEST HAT EVER!

MATERIALS

- Approx 120(125)yd/110(114)m heavy worsted weight yarn
- 5.75mm (size 10 U.S.) dpn and 16"/41 and 24"/61cm *or size to obtain gauge*
- Stitch marker
- Darning needle

GAUGE

16 sts = 4"/10cm

Always check gauge.

CROWN

Using dpn, CO 12 sts and divide among 3 dpn, *or* do the Wrap Method described on page 14.

Rnd 1 and all odd rnds: K.

Rnd 2: *k1, m1,* repeat around— 18 sts total.

Rnd 4: *k2, m1,* repeat around— 24 sts total.

Rnd 6: *k3, m1,* repeat around— 30 sts total.

Repeat rnds 1 and 2, each time adding an additional k st before each m1 until there are 10(11) k sts before each m1— 72(78) sts total.

Switch to cn (16"/41cm for *Medium,* 24"/61cm for *Large*); pm to denote beg/end of the rnd.

K for 9(9½)"/23(24)cm from crown.

BO loosely.

FINISHING

Sew in all ends.

This hat was knit with: Classic Elite's *Beatrice,* 100% wool, 1¾/50g = 63yd/58m

Large (on model)
2 balls, color #3250 (mountain meadow)

VARIATION

Using bulky weight yarn really beefs up the texture.

MATERIALS

- Approx 105(110)yd/96(101)m bulky weight yarn
- 9mm (size 13 U.S.) dpn and 24"/61cm cn *or size to obtain gauge*
- Stitch marker
- Darning needle

GAUGE

8 sts = 4"/10cm

Always check gauge.

CROWN

Using dpn, CO 12 sts and divide among 3 dpn, *or* do the Wrap Method described on page 14.

Rnd 1 and all odd rnds: K.

Rnd 2: *k1, m1,* repeat around— 18 sts total.

Rnd 4: *k2, m1,* repeat around— 24 sts total.

Rnd 6: *k3, m1,* repeat around— 30 sts total.

Repeat rnds 1 and 2, each time adding an additional k st before each m1 until there are 5(6) k sts before each m1— 42(48) sts total.

Switch to cn (16"/41cm for *Medium,* 24"/61cm for *Large*); pm to denote beg/end of the rnd.

K for 9(9½)"/23(24)cm from crown.

BO loosely.

FINISHING

Sew in all ends.

This hat was knit with: Rowan's *Biggy Print,* 100% wool, 3½oz/100g = 33yd/30m

Medium
2 balls, color #246 (razzle dazzle)
or
2 balls, color #253 (joker)

BULKY WEIGHT NINA
IN RAZZLE DAZZLE

BULKY WEIGHT
NINA IN JOKER

Buckets and Boxes

Just because you're knitting

"in-the-round" doesn't mean you're limited to rounded shapes. The patterns in this section feature the flat tops and boxy silhouettes that you're accustomed to seeing in hats made from felt or other more rigid materials. When you knit them, they're flexible, both in form and style; they can be rolled up to fit in the pocket, and can be worn with anything from jeans to a formal coat.

SKILL LEVEL

Easy

SIZE

Medium
20 to 21"/51 to 53cm

Large
22 to 23"/56 to 58cm

A BIT OF A FLIRT, THIS EYELASH-TRIMMED, FLARED-BRIMMED HAT GOES EASILY FROM CITY TO COUNTRY AND BACK AGAIN. EXTRA TEXTURE AND COLOR NUANCE CAN BE ACHIEVED BY BLENDING YARNS FROM THE SAME COLOR FAMILY.

MATERIALS

- Color A: Approx 45(50)yd/41(46)m bulky weight chenille yarn
- Color B: Approx 60(70)yd/54(64)m eyelash yarn
- 8mm (size 11 U.S.) dpn and 24"/61cm cn *or size to obtain gauge*
- Stitch marker
- Darning needle

GAUGE

8 sts = 4"/10cm

Always check gauge.

VERA

CROWN

Using dpn and A, CO 12 sts and divide among 3 dpn *or* do the Wrap Method described on page 14.

Rnd 1 and all odd rnds: K.

Rnd 2: *k1, m1,* repeat around—18 sts total.

Rnd 4: *k2, m1,* repeat around—24 sts total.

Rnd 6: *k3, m1,* repeat around—30 sts total.

Repeat rnds 1 and 2, each time adding an addtional k st before each m1, until there are 4(5) k sts before each m1—36(42) sts total.

Switch to cn; pm to denote beg/end of rnd.

K 1 rnd.

TURN OF CROWN

P 3 rnds.

RISE

K for 3 3/4(4)"/10(10.5)cm.

BRIM

Attach B and with A:

k 3, t1, repeat around.

K 4 rnds.

BO loosely.

FINISHING

Sew in all ends.

This hat was knit: with Lion Brand's *Thick & Quick Chenille,* 91% acrylic/9% rayon, 75yd/69m and Lion Brand's Fun Fur, 100% polyester, 1³/₄oz/50g = 60yd/54m

Medium

Color A: 1 ball, Chenille, color #215 (sapphire print)

Color B: 1 ball, Fun Fur, color #320 (sapphire)

Large (on model)

Color A: 1 ball, Chenille, color #281 (jewel print)

Color B: 1 ball, Fun Fur, color #179 (peacock)

VERA IN SAPPHIRE AND SAPPHIRE PRINT

VITA

SKILL LEVEL

Intermediate

SIZE

Medium
20 to 21"/51 to 53cm
Large
22 to 23"/56 to 58cm

A ROLLED BRIM, FLAT-TOP HAT

FLATTERS AND FRAMES THE FACE WHILE KEEPING THE EARS COVERED AND WARM. VITA IS STYLED MUCH LIKE NONA (SEE PAGE 60), THE BIG DIFFERENCE BEING THE BRIM. VITA'S BRIM COMES STRAIGHT DOWN, HUGGING THE HEAD, WHEREAS THE NONA FLARES SLIGHTLY AT THE BOTTOM.

MATERIALS

- Color A: Approx 110(120)yd/100(110)m bulky weight yarn
- Color B: 88yd/80m bulky weight blend of mohair, wool, and nylon
- 8mm (size 11 U.S.) dpn and 16"/41cm and 24"/61cm cn *or size to obtain gauge*
- Stitch marker
- Darning needle

GAUGE

10 sts = 4"/10cm

Always check gauge.

CROWN

Using dpn and Color A, CO 12 sts and divide among 3 dpn *or* do the Wrap Method described on page 14.

Rnd 1 and all odd rnds: K.

Rnd 2: *k1, m1,* repeat around— 18 sts total.

Rnd 4: *k2, m1,* repeat around— 24 sts total.

Rnd 6: *k3, m1,* repeat around— 30 sts total.

Repeat rnds 1 and 2, each time adding an additional k st before each m1, until there are 6(7) k sts before each m1— 48(54) sts total.

K 1 rnd.

Switch to cn (16″/41cm for Medium, 24″/61cm for Large); pm to denote beg/end of rnd.

TURN OF CROWN

P 3 rnds.

RISE

Attach color B and K for 6″/15cm.

BO loosely.

FINISHING

Sew in all ends.

This hat was knit with: Classic Elite's *Tigress,* 100% wool, 7oz/200g = 181yd/165m and Classic Elite's *Phoenix,* 32% mohair/8% wool/52%nylon/8%nylon, $1^3/_4$oz/50g =88yd/80m

Medium (on background model)

1 ball, *Tigress,* color # 7085 (bengal)

1 ball, *Phoenix,* color #6675 (goose down)

(on model)

1 ball, *Tigress,* color #7003 (tabby)

1 ball, *Phoenix,* color #6676 (teddy bear)

BULKY WEIGHT
VITA IN TABBY
AND TEDDY BEAR

VARIATIONS

This yarn choice shows off the brim and rise.

MATERIALS

- Approx 80(90)yd/73(82)m bulky weight yarn
- 9mm (size 13 U.S.) dpn and 16"/41cm and 24"/61cm cn *or size to obtain gauge*
- Stitch marker
- Darning needle

GAUGE

8 sts = 4"/10cm

Always check gauge.

CROWN

Using dpn, CO 12 sts and divide among 3 dpn *or* do the Wrap Method described on page 14.

Rnd 1 and all odd rnds: K.

Rnd 2: *k1, m1,* repeat around—18 sts total.

Rnd 4: *k2, m1,* repeat around—24 sts total.

Rnd 6: *k3, m1,* repeat around—30 sts total.

Repeat rnds 1 and 2, each time adding an additional k st before each m1, until there are 4(5) k sts before each m1—36(42) sts total.

For Medium:

K8, m1, repeat 3x more—40 sts total.

For Large:

K20, m1, repeat 1x more—44 sts total.

K 1 rnd.

Switch to cn (16"/41cm for Medium, 24"/61cm for Large); pm to denote beg/end of rnd.

TURN OF CROWN

P 3 rnds.

RISE

K for 6"/15cm.

BO loosely.

FINISHING

Sew in all ends.

This hat was knit with: Blue Sky Alpacas' *Bulky Alpaca,* 50% alpaca/50% wool, 3½oz/100g =45yd/41m

Medium

2 balls, color #1005 (fawn)

Large

1 ball, color #1010 (rust)

BULKY WEIGHT
VITA IN FAWN

BULKY WEIGHT
VITA IN RUST

SKILL LEVEL

Intermediate

SIZE

Medium
20 to 21"/51 to 53cm

Large
22 to 23"/56 to 58cm

DUNCAN

THIS HAT HAS A TEXTURED, HIGH RISE

WITH A ROLLED BRIM. THE HORIZONTAL PATTERN IS THE DESIGN INTEREST IN THE HAT AND AFTER YOU MAKE ONE, YOU MIGHT WANT TO EXPERIMENT BY TRYING ANOTHER STITCH PATTERN ON THE RISE.

MATERIALS

- Approx 115(120)yd/105(110)m chunky weight yarn
- 5.75mm (size 10 U.S.) dpn and 24"/61cm cn *or size to obtain gauge*
- Stitch marker
- Darning needle

GAUGE

12 sts = 4"/10cm

Always check gauge.

CROWN

Using dpn, CO 12 sts and divide among 3 dpn *or* do the Wrap Method described on page 14.

Rnd 1 and all odd rnds: K.

Rnd 2: *k1, m1,* repeat around—18 sts total.

Rnd 4: *k2, m1,* repeat around—24 sts total.

Rnd 6: *k3, m1,* repeat around—30 sts total.

Repeat rnds 1 and 2, each time adding an additional k st before each m1, until there are 8(9) k sts before each m1—60(66) sts total.

Switch to cn; pm to denote beg/end of rnd.

TURN OF CROWN

P 3 rnds.

RISE

K 2 rnds.

P 1 rnd.

Repeat last 3 rnds 7x more.

BRIM

K3, m1, repeat around, ending k 0(2) sts.

K 5 rnds.

BO loosely.

FINISHING

Sew in all ends.

This hat was knit with: Classic Elite's *Gatsby,* 70% wool/15% viscose/15% nylon, 3½oz/100g = 94yd/86m

Medium (on model)
2 balls, color #2145 (chai latte)

Large
2 balls, color #2175 (earl grey)

DUNCAN IN
EARL GREY

BOBBI

SKILL LEVEL

Intermediate

SIZE

Medium
20 to 21"/51 to 53cm

Large
22 to 23"/56 to 58cm

AT FIRST GLANCE,

MAKING THE BOBBLES ON THIS CHARMING PILLBOX MAY SEEM LIKE A COMPLICATED AND TIME-CONSUMING PROCESS. BUT GIVE IT A TRY—YOU'LL FIND THAT THEY'RE FUN TO MAKE AND THE TEXTURE THEY ADD TO YOUR DESIGN IS WELL WORTH THE EFFORT.

MATERIALS

- Approx 120(130)yd/ 110(119)m heavy worsted weight yarn
- 5.25mm (size 9 U.S.) dpn and 16"/41cm cn *or size to obtain gauge*
- Stitch marker
- Darning needle

GAUGE

16 sts = 4"/10 cm

Always check gauge.

MAKE BOBBLE (MB)

To make a bobble, k into a st 6 times, pulling up the new sts starting at the back and alternating to the front. You will end up with a cluster of sts on your right-hand needle. Starting with the outmost st on the right side of the cluster, pull the st over all the others, dropping it as you go, and repeat this with every subsequent st until only 1 st remains. Sl st this last st onto the left needle and knit it. That completes the bobble.

CROWN

Using dpn, CO 12 sts and divide among 3 dpn or do the Wrap Method described on page 14.

Rnd 1 and all odd rnds: K.

Rnd 2: *k1, m1,* repeat around—18 sts total.

Rnd 4: *k2, m1,* repeat around—24 sts total.

Rnd 6: *k3, m1,* repeat around—30 sts total.

Repeat rnds 1 and 2, each time adding an additional k st before each m1, until there are 10(11) sts before each m1 st—72(78) sts total.

K 1 rnd.

Switch to cn; pm to denote beg/end of rnd.

TURN OF CROWN

P 3 rnds.

RISE

Rnd 1: K.

Rnd 2: k0(2)tog, k around—72(77) sts remain.

Rnd 3: k0(3), k0(2)tog, k around—72(76) sts remain.

Rnd 4: *k3, MB,* repeat around.

Rnds 5 to 7: K.

Rnd 8: k2, *MB, k3* repeat around, end MB, k1.

Rnds 9 to 11: K.

Rnd 12: k1, *MB, k3* repeat around, end MB, k2.

Rnds 13 to 15: K.

Rnd 16: *MB, k3,* repeat around.

Rnds 17 to 19: K.

Rnd 20: Repeat rnd 4.

Rnds 21 to 23: K.

BRIM

P 6 rnds.

BO loosely.

FINISHING

Sew in all ends.

This hat was knit with: Blue Sky Alpacas' *Heavy Worsted Alpaca*, 50% alpaca/50% wool, 3 1/2 oz/100g = 100yd/91m

Large (on model)

2 balls, color #2008 (pink)

Medium

2 balls, color #2005 (butter)

BOBBI IN BUTTER

SKILL LEVEL

Experienced

SIZE

Medium
20 to 21"/51 to 53cm

Large
22 to 23"/56 to 58cm

THIS HAT FORM IS SIMPLE—

ITS CHALLENGE LIES IN MANIPULATING THE TEXTURED YARN. THE KEY IS TO WORK SLOWLY AND ALLOW THE YARN A LOT OF "GIVE" TO ACCOMMODATE THE TEXTURE. THE TWO YARNS WORK TOGETHER TO CREATE A PIECE OF FABRIC THAT HARDLY APPEARS KNITTED AND IS EXTREMELY INTERESTING TO LOOK AT.

MATERIALS

- Color A: Approx 60(70)yd/55(64)m chunky weight yarn
- Color B: Approx 60(70)yd/55(64)m worsted weight novelty yarn
- 8mm (size 11 U.S.) dpn and 24"/61cm cn *or size to obtain gauge*
- Stitch marker
- Darning needle

GAUGE

8 sts (with A and B together) = 4"/10cm

Always check gauge.

CROWN

Using dpn and holding a strand each of A and B together, CO 12 sts and divide among 3 dpn *or* do the Wrap Method described on page 14.

Rnd 1 and all odd rnds: K.

Rnd 2: *k1, m1,* repeat around— 18 sts total.

Rnd 4: *k2, m1,* repeat around— 24 sts total.

Rnd 6: *k3, m1,* repeat around— 30 sts total.

Repeat rnds 1 and 2, each time adding an additional k st before each m1, until there are 4(5) sts before each m1— 36(42) sts total.

K 1 rnd.

Switch to cn; pm to denote beg/end of rnd.

For *Large,* skp to Turn of Crown; For *Medium*

K 11, m1, repeat 2x more—39 sts total.

K 1 rnd.

TURN OF CROWN

P 2 rnds.

RISE

K for 4"/10cm.

P 2 rnds.

Turn work to WS and BO loosely.

FINISHING

Use A to sew the bottom end together. Sew in all ends.

This hat was knit with: Classic Elite's *Parade,* 82% nylon/18% acrylic, 1¾oz/50g = 33yd/30m and Classic Elite's *Paintbox,* 100% wool, 1¾oz/50g = 55/yd/50m

Large (on model)

Color A: 2 balls, *Parade,* color #4547 (Chinese New Year)

Color B: 2 balls, *Paintbox,* color #6830 (cobalt violet)

LARA

SKILL LEVEL

Easy

SIZE

Medium
20 to 21"/51 to 53cm

Large
22 to 23"/56 to 58cm

THIS HAT IS STYLED AFTER THE UNFORGETTABLE FUZZY BLACK PERSIAN-LAMB PILLBOX HAT JULIE CHRISTIE WORE AS LARA, THE FEMME FATALE IN THE EPIC FILM **DR. ZHIVAGO**. YOUR KNITTED VERSION WILL BE EQUALLY MEMO-RABLE, DESPITE THE FACT THAT IT'S QUITE SIMPLE TO MAKE.

MATERIALS

- Color A: Approx 70(80)yd/64(73)m bulky weight yarn

- Color B: Approx 70(80)yd/64(73)m eyelash yarn

- 8mm (size 11 U.S.) dpn and 16"/41cm and 24"/61cm cn *or size to obtain gauge*

- Stitch marker

- Darning needle

GAUGE

8 sts (with A and B together) = 4"/10cm

Always check gauge.

CROWN

Using dpn and holding A and B together, CO 12 sts and divide among 3 dpn *or* do the Wrap Method described on page 14.

Rnd 1 and all odd rnds: K.

Rnd 2: *k1, m1,* repeat around— 18 sts total.

Rnd 4: *k2, m1,* repeat around— 24 sts total.

Rnd 6: *k3, m1,* repeat around— 30 sts total.

Repeat rnds 1 and 2, each time adding an additional k st before each m1 until there are 4(5) sts before each m1 st— 36(42) sts total.

Switch to cn (16"/41cm for Medium, 24"/61cm for Large); pm to denote beg/end of rnd.

K 1 rnd.

For *Large,* skp to turn of crown; For *Medium:*

k11, m1, repeat 2x more— 39 sts total.

K 1 rnd.

TURN OF CROWN

P 2 rnds.

RISE

K for 4 1/2(4 3/4)"/11(12)cm.

P 2 rnds.

Turn work to WS, BO loosely.

Note: Working the BO on the WS allows the edge to curl inward readily.

FINISHING

Sew in all ends.

This hat was knit with: Lion Brand's *Thick & Quick Chenille,* 91% acrylic/9% rayon, 100yd/9m and Lion Brand's *Fun Fur,* 100% polyester, 1 3/4 oz/50g = 60yd/54m

Large (on model)

1 ball, *Chenille,* color #195 (fuchsia)

1 ball, *Fun Fur,* color #3994 (fuchsia)

SKILL LEVEL

Intermediate

SIZE

Medium
20 to 21"/51 to 53cm

Large
22 to 23"/56 to 58cm

HERE'S ANOTHER DR. ZHIVAGO-INSPIRED

TOPPER. THIS EYELASH-COVERED
PILLBOX CALLS TO MIND THE ONE
WORN BY GERALDINE O'NEILL AS
SHE EXITED A TRAIN IN A FABULOUS
BABY-PINK OUTFIT TO GREET THE
GORGEOUS OMAR SHARIF.

MATERIALS

- Color A: Approx
  120(125)yd/110(114)m chunky
  weight yarn
- Color B: Approx
  80(85)yd/73(78)m eyelash yarn
- 6.50mm (size 10 1/2 U.S.) dpn
  and 16"/41cm and 24"/61cm cn
  or size to obtain gauge
- Stitch marker
- Darning needle

GAUGE

12 sts = 4"/10cm

Always check gauge.

CROWN

Using dpn and A, CO 12 sts and divide among 3 dpn *or* do the Wrap Method described on page 14.

Rnd 1 and all odd rnds: K.

Rnd 2: *k1, m1,* repeat around—18 sts total.

Rnd 4: *k2, m1,* repeat around—24 sts total.

Rnd 6: *k3, m1,* repeat around—30 sts total.

Repeat rnds 1 and 2, each time adding an additional k st before each m1 until there are 7(8) sts before each m1—54(60) sts total.

K 1 rnd.

Switch to cn (16"/41cm for *Medium,* 24"/61 for *Large*); pm to denote beg/end of rnd.

K 17(19), m1, repeat 2x more—57(63) sts total.

K 1 rnd.

TURN OF CROWN

Turn work to WS, k 1 rnd.

RISE

With WS facing, and with A and B together, k for 5"/13cm.

With A only, k 1 rnd.

BO loosely in k1/p1 rib.

FINISHING

Sew in all ends.

This hat was knit with: Brown Sheep's *Lamb's Pride Bulky,* 85% wool/15% mohair, 4oz/113g = 125yd/114m and Berroco's *Sizzle Bright,* 95% polyester/5% nylon, 1¾oz/50g = 92yd/85m

Medium

Color A: 1 ball, *Lamb's Pride Bulky,* color #M-34 (Victorian pink)

Color B: 1 ball, *Sizzle Bright,* color #1661 (orchid)

Or (on model)

Color A: 1 ball, *Lamb's Pride Bulky,* color #M-01 (sandy heather)

Color B: 1 ball, *Sizzle Bright,* color #1697 (moonstone)

Large

Color A: 1 ball, *Lamb's Pride Bulky,* color #M-102 (orchid thistle)

Color B: 1 ball, *Sizzle Bright,* color #1646 (purple passion)

or

Color A: 1 ball, *Lamb's Pride Bulky,* color #M-04 (charcoal heather)

Color B: 1 ball, *Sizzle Bright,* color #1612 (black)

TONYA (LEFT TO RIGHT): IN CHARCOAL HEATHER AND BLACK, PINK AND ORCHID, ORCHID THISTLE AND PURPLE PASSION

NESSA

NAMED AFTER VIRGINIA WOOLF'S SISTER, VANESSA BELL (A TALENTED NEEDLEPOINTER), THIS HAT HAS A REVERSE STOCKINGNETTE-STITCH RISE AND LOTS OF FLAIR, LIKE ITS NAMESAKE.

MATERIALS

- Approx 70(80)yd/64(73)m bulky weight yarn
- 9mm (size 13 U.S.) dpn and 24"/61cm cn *or size to obtain gauge*
- Stitch marker
- Darning needle

GAUGE

8 sts = 4"/10cm

Always check gauge.

CROWN

Using dpn, CO 12 sts and divide among 3 dpn, *or* do the Wrap Method described on page 14.

Rnd 1 and all odd rnds: K.

Rnd 2: *k1, m1,* repeat around— 18 sts total.

Rnd 4: *k2, m1,* repeat around— 24 sts total.

Rnd 6: *k3, m1,* repeat around— 30 sts total.

Repeat rnds 1 and 2, each time adding an additional k st before each m1, until there are 4(5) sts before each m1— 36(42) sts total.

K 1 rnd.

NESSA IN
KHAKI AND
CREAM

RISE

With WS facing, k for 6"/15cm. BO loosely.

FINISHING

Sew in all ends.

This hat was knit with: Brown Sheep's *Burley Spun*, 100% wool, 8oz/226g = 132yd/121m and Brown Sheep's *Lamb's Pride Bulky*, 85% wool/15% mohair, 4oz/113g =125yd/114m

Medium (on model)

1 ball, color #BS181 (prairie fire)

1 ball, color #M-115 (oatmeal)

Large

1 ball, color #BS10 (cream)

1 ball, color #M-18 (khaki)

VARIATION

A solid color yarn accentuates the width of the brim.

MATERIALS

- Approx 80(90)yd/73(82)m bulky weight yarn
- 6.50mm (size 10 1/2 U.S.) dpn and 16"/41cm cn *or size to obtain gauge*
- Stitch marker
- Darning needle

GAUGE

10 sts = 4"/10cm

Always check gauge.

CROWN

Using dpn, CO 12 sts and divide among 3 dpn, *or* do the Wrap Method described on page 14.

Rnd 1 and all odd rnds: K.

Rnd 2: *k1, m1,* repeat around—18 sts total.

Rnd 4: *k2, m1,* repeat around—24 sts total.

Rnd 6: *k3, m1,* repeat around—30 sts total.

Repeat rnds 1 and 2, each time adding an additional k st before each m1, until there are 5(6) sts before each m1—42 (48) sts total.

K 1 rnd.

For *Medium,* skp to Rise; For *Large*

K13 (15), m1, repeat 2x more—45 (51) sts total.

Switch to cn; pm to denote the beg/end of rnd.

K 1 rnd.

RISE

With WS facing, k for 6´/15cm. BO loosely.

FINISHING

Sew in all ends.

This hat was knit with: Tahki Stacy Charles' *Baby,* 100% wool, 3 1/2oz/100g = 60yd/55m

Medium

2 balls, color #16 (black)

Large

2 balls, color #12 (fuchsia)

NESSA IN BLACK

NESSA IN FUCHSIA

DAMIEN

ADD SOME RAZZLE-DAZZLE

TO THE PILLBOX STYLE BY KNITTING BEADS INTO THE RISE. IT'S EASIER TO DO THAN IT LOOKS — JUST FOLLOW THE INSTRUCTIONS ON PAGE 22.

MATERIALS

- Approx 120(135)yd/110(123)m chunky weight yarn
- 150(175) pony beads or any bead with a similar-size hole
- 5.7mm (size 10 U.S.) dpn and 16"/41cm and 24"/61cm cn *or size to obtain gauge*
- Darning needle
- Stitch marker

GAUGE

12 sts = 4"/10cm

Always check gauge.

PREPARATION

Using a darning needle, string all the pony beads for your hat size onto the yarn.

CROWN

Using dpn, CO 12 sts and divide among 3 dpn *or* do the Wrap Method described on page 14.

Rnd 1 and all odd rnds: K.

Rnd 2: *k1, m1,* repeat around—18 sts total.

Rnd 4: *k2, m1,* repeat around—24 sts total.

Rnd 6: *k3, m1,* repeat around—30 sts total.

Repeat rnds 1 and 2, each time adding an additional k st before each m1, until there are 9(10) sts before each m1—66(72) sts total.

K 1 rnd. Switch to cn (16"/41cm for Medium, 24"/61cm for Large); pm to denote beg/end of the rnd.

TURN OF CROWN

P 2 rnds.

K 1 rnd.

RISE

Rnd 4: *k5, k1 with a bead,* repeat around.

Rnd 5: K. Note: Ktbl in the stitches holding the beads.

Rnd 6: k2, *k1 with a bead, k5,* repeat around, k3.

Rnd 7: K. Note: Ktbl in the stitches holding the beads.

Repeat rnds 4 to 7, until piece measures 4 1/2"/11cm; end with a k rnd.

P 4 rnds.

BO loosely.

FINISHING

Sew in all ends. Turn brim hem inward and upward and baste loosely.

This hat was knit with: Classic Elite's *Two.Two,* 100% wool, 3 1/2 oz/100g = 110yd/100m

Medium

1 ball, color #1513 (black)

Pony beads, #6 (crystal)

or

1 ball, color #1560 (heather forest)

Pony beads, #345 (Americana multi)

Large

1 ball, color #1516 (neutral)

Pony beads, #345 (Americana multi)

Or (on model)

1 ball, color #1504 (turquoise)

Pony beads in black, white, and red

DAMIEN (LEFT TO RIGHT): IN BLACK WITH CRYSTAL BEADS, HEATHER FOREST WITH MULTICOLORED BEADS, NEUTRAL WITH MULTICOLORED BEADS

SKILL LEVEL

Intermediate

SIZE

Medium
20 to 21"/51 to 53cm

Large
22 to 23"/56 to 58cm

THIS SEED-STITCH PILLBOX

HAS A CHARMING ELEGANCE WITHOUT BEING TOO FORMAL. IT'S IMPORTANT TO USE A SMOOTH, NON-TEXTURED YARN (I.E., NO BOUCLÉS) WITH THIS PATTERN SO THAT THE SEEDED TEXTURE REALLY POPS OUT.

MATERIALS

- Approx 120(125)yd/110(114)m bulky weight yarn
- 6.50mm (size 10 1/2 U.S.) dpn and 24"/61cm cn *or size to obtain gauge*
- Stitch marker
- Darning needle

GAUGE

12 sts = 4" /10cm

Always check gauge.

CROWN

Using dpn, CO 12 sts and divide among 3 dpn *or* do the Wrap Method described on page 14.

Rnd 1 and all odd rnds: K.

Rnd 2: *k1, m1,* repeat around—18 sts total.

Rnd 4: *k2, m1,* repeat around—24 sts total.

Rnd 6: *k3, m1,* repeat around—30 sts total.

Repeat rnds 1 and 2, each time adding an additional k st before each m1 until there are 8(9) k sts before each m1—60(66) sts total.

K 1 rnd.

TURN OF CROWN

P 2 rnds.

RISE

Rnd 1: K.

Rnd 2: *k1, p1,* repeat around.

Rnd 3: *p1, k1,* repeat around.

Repeat rnds 2 and 3 for 4"/10cm. P 4 rnds.

BO loosely by purling.

FINISHING

Sew in all ends.

> This hat was knit with: Brown Sheep's *Lamb's Pride Bulky,* 85% wool/15% mohair, 4 oz/113g = 125yd/114m

Medium (on model)

1 ball, color #M-18 (khaki)

Large

1 ball, color #M-59 (periwinkle)

VARIATION

Use larger needles to create a different look.

MATERIALS

- Approx 90(110)yd/82(101)m bulky weight yarn
- 8mm (size 11 U.S.) dpn and 24"/61cm cn *or size to obtain gauge*
- Stitch marker
- Darning needle

GAUGE

10 sts = 4"/10cm

Always check gauge.

CROWN

Using dpn, CO 12 sts and divide among 3 dpn *or* do the Wrap Method described on page 14.

Rnd 1 and all odd rnds: K.

Rnd 2: *k1, m1,* repeat around—18 sts total.

Rnd 4: *k2, m1,* repeat around—24 sts total.

Rnd 6: *k3, m1,* repeat around—30 sts total.

Repeat rnds 1 and 2, each time adding an additional k st before each m1 until there are 5 k sts before each m1—42 sts total. K 1 rnd.

For *Medium,* skp to turn of crown.

For *Large,* *K6, m1, k13, m1,* —repeat once more—46 sts total.

K 1 rnd.

Switch to cn; pm to denote beg/end of rnd.

TURN OF CROWN

P 2 rnds.

RISE

Rnd 1: K.

Rnd 2: *k1, p1,* repeat around.

Rnd 3: *p1, k1,* repeat around.

Repeat rnds 2 and 3 for 4"/10cm.

BO loosely by purling.

FINISHING

Sew in all ends.

> This hat was knit with: Blue Sky Alpacas' *Bulky Alpaca,* 50% wool/50% alpaca, 3½ oz/100g = 45yd/41m

Medium

2 balls, color #1010 (rust)

Large

2 balls, color #1018 (pink)

VIOLET SEED IN PERIWINKLE

VIOLET SEED IN RUST

VIOLET SEED IN PINK

SKILL LEVEL

Intermediate

SIZE

Medium
20 to 21"/51 to 53cm

Large
22 to 23"/56 to 58cm

ARCHITECTURAL IN FORM,

YET SENSUOUS AND CURVY,
THIS VERSATILE HAT SUITS
BOTH MEN AND WOMEN. IT
ALSO COMPLEMENTS BOTH
CONTEMPORARY AND TRADI-
TIONAL WARDROBES.

VALERY

MATERIALS

■ Color A: Approx 45(55)yd/41(40)m bulky weight yarn

■ Color B: Approx 45(55)yd/41(40)m bulky weight yarn

■ 8mm (size 11 U.S.) dpn and 16"/41cm and 24"/61cm cn *or size to obtain gauge*

■ Stitch marker

■ Darning needle

GAUGE

■ 10 sts = 4"/10cm

Always check gauge.

CROWN

Using dpn and A, CO 12 sts and divide among 3 dpn, *or* do the Wrap Method described on page 14.

Rnd 1 and all odd rnds: K.

Rnd 2: *k1, m1,* repeat around— 18 sts total.

Rnd 4: *k2, m1,* repeat around— 24 sts total.

Rnd 6: *k3, m1,* repeat around— 30 sts total.

Repeat rnds 1 and 2, each time adding an additional k st before each m1, until there are 6(7) sts before each m1— 48(54) sts.

K 1 rnd.

Switch to cn (16"/41cm for Medium, 24"/61cm for Large); pm to denote beg/end of rnd.

TURN OF CROWN AND RISE

With B: K 1 rnd.

P 5 rnds.

With color A: K 5 rnds.

With color B: K 1 rnd.

P 5 rnds.

With color A: K 5 rnds.

With color B: K 1 rnd.

P 5 rnds.

With WS facing, BO loosely.

FINISHING

Sew in all ends.

This hat was knit with: Brown Sheep's *Burley Spun,* 100% wool, 8oz/226g = 132yd/121m

Medium (single color)

1 ball, color #BS115 (oatmeal)

Large (on models)

Color A: 1 ball, Burley Spun, #BS05 (onyx)

Color B: 1 ball, Burley Spun, #BS07 (sable)

VALERY IN OATMEAL

BERETS AND TAMS

A BERET OR TAM IS A STAPLE

OF ANY HAT WARDROBE. THE PATTERNS IN THIS
SECTION SHOW JUST HOW VERSATILE THIS
CLASSIC STYLE CAN BE. MOVE BEYOND BASIC
BLACK AND ADD TEXTURE, STRIPES OF COLOR,
OR A TASSEL ON THE TOP FOR A PLAYFUL
TOUCH. USE UNEXPECTED YARNS OR ADD
INTERESTING DETAILS, SUCH AS A RIBBED BRIM.

SKILL LEVEL

Intermediate

SIZE

Medium
20 to 21"/51 to 53cm

Large
22 to 23"/56 to 58cm

THE HEAVILY TEXTURED CAL

IS NOTHING IF NOT PLAYFUL. IT TAKES TWO STRANDS—ONE OF MONTERA AND THE OTHER OF LOULOU. EXPERIMENT WITH OTHER TEXTURE COMBINATIONS AS WELL (MAKE SURE THE COMBINED STRAND WILL GIVE YOU THE SAME GAUGE).

MATERIALS

- Color A: Approx 115(120)yd/100(110)m sport weight yarn
- Color B: Approx 65(75)yds/59(69)m novelty chunky weight yarn
- 5.75mm (size 10 U.S.) dpn and 24"/61cm cn *or size to obtain gauge*
- Stitch marker
- Darning needle

GAUGE

12 sts (with A and B together) = 4"/10cm

Always check gauge.

CROWN

Using dpn and holding one strand each of A and B together, CO 12 sts and divide among 3 dpn, or do the Wrap Method described on page 14.

Rnd 1 and all odd rnds: K.

Rnd 2: *k1, m1,* repeat around—18 sts total.

Rnd 4: *k2, m1,* repeat around—24 sts total.

Rnd 6: *k3, m1,* repeat around—30 sts total.

Repeat rnds 1 and 2, adding a k st before each m1, until there are 12(13) sts before each m1 st—84(90) sts total.

K 1 rnd.

Switch to cn; pm to denote beg/end of rnd.

K 2 rnds.

BRIM

Rnd 1 and every odd rnd: K.

Rnd 2: *k12(13), k2tog,* repeat around—78(84) sts remain.

Rnd 4: *k11(12), k2tog,* repeat around—72(78) sts remain.

Rnd 6: *k10(11), k2tog,* repeat around—66(72) sts remain.

Cut B and with A only:

For *Medium:* (k6, k2tog) 3x, (k5, k2tog) 6x—57 sts remain.

For *Large:* *k7, k2tog,* repeat around—64 sts remain.

P 7 rnds.

BO loosely.

FINISHING

Sew in all ends.

Tip: For extra texture, gently push the novelty yarn pompoms on the inside of the hat to the outside using the pointed end of a knitting needle.

This hat was knit with: Classic Elite's *Montera,* 50% llama/50% wool, 3½oz/100g = 127yd/116m and Classic Elite's *LouLou,* 83% wool/ 17% acrylic, 1¾oz/50g = 80yd/73m

Medium (on model)

Color A: 1 ball, *Montera,* color #3819 (pink)

Color B: 1 ball, *LouLou,* color #1716 (natural)

Large

Color A: 1 ball, *Montera,* color #3887 (pear)

Color B: 1 ball, *LouLou,* color #1750 (Gigi's green)

CAL IN PEAR
AND GREEN

TAMI

SKILL LEVEL

Intermediate

SIZE

Medium
20 to 21"/51 to 53cm

Large
22 to 23"/56 to 58cm

THE FRENCH CALL IT A BERET;

THE SCOTS CALL IT A TAM.
WHATEVER YOU CHOOSE TO
CALL IT, YOU'LL LOVE THE
CLASSIC STYLING AND THE
CHEERY POMPOM ON TOP.

MATERIALS

- Color A: Approx 135(145)yd/123(133)m chunky weight yarn
- Color B: Approx 60yd/55m heavy worsted weight yarn
- 5.25mm (size 9 U.S.) and 5.75mm (size 10 U.S.) dpn and 16"/41 and 24"/61cm cn *or size to obtain gauge*
- Stitch marker
- Darning needle

GAUGE

Top: 12 sts = 4"/10cm

Brim ribbing: 16 sts = 4"/10cm

Always check gauge.

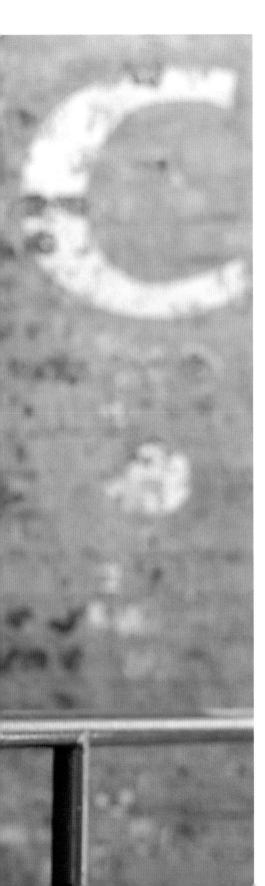

CROWN

Using 5.75 mm (size 10 U.S.) dpn and A, CO 12 sts and divide among 3 dpn *or* do Wrap Method described on page 14.

Rnd 1 and all odd rnds: K.

Rnd 2: *k1, m1,* repeat around— 18 sts total.

Rnd 4: *k2, m1,* repeat around— 24 sts total.

Rnd 6: *k3, m1,* repeat around— 30 sts total.

Repeat rnds 1 and 2, each time adding an additional k st before the m1 st until there are 11(12) k sts before each m1— 78(84) sts total.

K 2 rnds.

Switch to cn (16"/41cm for Medium, 24"/61cm for Large); pm to denote beg/end of rnd.

TURN OF CROWN

P 2 rnds.

BRIM

Rnds 1 and 2 and all even rnds: K.

Rnd 3: *k11(12), k2tog,* repeat around—72(78) sts remain.

Rnd 5: *k10(11), k2tog,* repeat around—66(72) sts remain.

Rnd 7: *k9(10), k2tog,* repeat around—60(66) sts remain.

RIBBED BAND

K 1 rnd.

Using 5.25 mm (size 9 U.S.) dpn and B:

k4, m1, repeat around, end k0(1) st— 72(80) sts total.

K1/p1 rib for 6 rnds.

BO loosely in k1/p1 rib.

FINISHING

Sew in all ends.

Using color B, make and attach a 5"/13cm-diameter pompom or tassel (see instructions on page 29) to the center top.

This hat was knit with: Classic Elite's *Bravo,* 40% rayon/13% silk/6% wool/6% nylon, 1³/₄oz/50g = 48yd/44m and Classic Elite's *Montera,* 50% wool/50% llama, 3¹/₂oz/100g = 127yd/116m

Medium (on model)

Color A: 2 balls, *Bravo,* color #3729 (Venetian rose)

Color B: 1 ball, *Montera,* color #3827 (cochineal)

Large

Color A: 2 balls, *Bravo,* color #3730 (garden)

Color B: 1 ball, *Montera,* color #3850 (glade green)

TAMI IN GARDEN AND GLADE GREEN

SIZE

Medium
20 to 21"/51 to 53cm

Large
22 to 23"/56 to 58cm

A TRADITIONAL BERET

WITH A TWIST, GLO
FEATURES ALTERNATING
STRIPES OF CONTRAST-
ING TEXTURE AND TRIM.

GLO

MATERIALS

- Color A: 60(70)yd/55(64)m chunky weight yarn
- Color B: 70(75)yd/64(69)m worsted weight yarn
- Color C: 55(75)yd/50(69)m chunky weight yarn
- 5.75mm (size 10 U.S.) dpn and 16"/41cm and 24"/61cm cn *or size to obtain gauge*
- Stitch marker
- Darning needle

GAUGE

Color A only: 14 sts = 4"/10cm

Color B and C (together): 12 sts = 4"/10cm

Always check gauge.

CROWN

Using dpn and A, CO 12 sts and divide among 3 dpn *or* do the Wrap Method described on page 14.

Rnd 1 and all odd rnds: K.

Rnd 2: *k1, m1,* repeat around—18 sts total.

Rnd 4: *k2, m1,* repeat around—24 sts total.

Rnd 6: *k3, m1,* repeat around—30 sts total.

With B and C:

Rnd 7 and all odd rnds: K.

Rnd 8: *k4, m1,* repeat around—36 sts total.

Rnd 10: *k5, m1,* repeat around—42 sts total.

Rnd 12: *k6, m1,* repeat around—48 sts total.

With A:

Rnd 13 and all odd rnds: K.

Rnd 14: *k7, m1,* repeat around—54 sts total.

Rnd 16: *k8, m1,* repeat around—60 sts total.

Rnd 18: *k9, m1,* repeat around—66 sts total.

Rnd 20: *k10, m1,* repeat around—72 sts total.

With B and C together:

Switch to cn (24"/61cm).

Rnd 21 and all rnds: K.

Rnd 22: *k11, m1,* repeat around—78 sts total.

Rnd 24: *k12, m1,* repeat around—84 sts total.

With A:

Rnd 25 and all odd rnds: K.

Rnd 26: *k13, m1,* repeat around—90 sts total.

Rnd 28: *k14, m1,* repeat around—96 sts total.

For *Medium*, skp to Turn of Crown ; For *Large*

Rnd 29, and all odd rnds: K.

Rnd 30: *k15, m1,* repeat around—102 sts total.

Rnd 32: *k16, m1,* repeat around—108 sts total.

TURN OF CROWN

With B and C together:

K 3 rnds.

BRIM

With A:

Rnd 1 and every odd rnd: K.

Rnd 2: *k14(16), k2tog,* repeat around—90(102) sts remain.

Rnd 4: *k13(15), k2tog,* repeat around—84 (96) sts remain.

Rnd 6: *k12(14), k2tog,* repeat around—78(90) sts remain.

Switch to cn (16"/41cm):

Rnd 7 and every odd rnd: K.

Rnd 8: *k11(13), k2tog,* repeat around—72(84) sts remain.

Rnd 10: *k10(12), k2tog,* repeat around—66(78) sts remain.

Rnd 12: For *Medium:* *k6, (k1, k2tog) 9x* repeat once more—48 sts remain. For *Large:* *k1, k2tog,* repeat around—52 sts remain.

BRIM EDGE

With B and C together, turn work and with WS facing: K 4 rnds.

BO loosely.

FINISHING

Sew in ends.

This hat was knit with: Classic Elite's *Montera,* 50% llama/50% wool, 3½oz/100g = 127yd/166m and Classic Elite's *Phoenix,* 32% mohair/8% wool/52% nylon/8% acrylic, 1¾oz/50g = 88yd/81m

Medium (on model)

Color A: 1 ball, *Montera,* color #3819 (rose quartz)

Color B: 1 ball, *Phoenix,* color #6676 (teddy bear)

Large

Color A: 1 ball, *Montera,* color #3852 (Peruvian potato)

Color B: 1 ball, *Phoenix,* color #6676 (teddy bear)

Color C: 1 ball, *Montera,* color #3819 (rose quartz)

GLO IN PERUVIAN POTATO, TEDDY BEAR AND ROSE QUARTZ

SKILL LEVEL
Beginner

SIZE
Medium
20 to 21"/51 to 53cm

Large
22 to 23"/56 to 58cm

BERETS ARE USUALLY MADE WITH THIN, DRAPEY YARN. THIS ONE, HOWEVER, GETS AWAY WITH DOUBLING THE YARN FOR A HEFTIER GAUGE BECAUSE THE ORIGINAL FIBER IS SOFT AND FLUFFY TO BEGIN WITH.

MATERIALS

- Approx 80(90)yd/73(82)m bulky weight yarn
- 8mm (size 11 U.S.) dpn and 24"/61cm cn *or size to obtain gauge*
- Stitch marker
- Darning needle

GAUGE

8 sts (with A and B together) = 4"/10cm

Always check gauge.

CROWN

Using dpn and two strands of yarn together, CO 12 sts and divide among 3 dpn *or* do the Wrap Method described on page 14.

Rnd 1 and all odd rnds: K.

Rnd 2: *k1, m1,* repeat around—18 sts total.

Rnd 4: *k2, m1,* repeat around—24 sts total.

Rnd 6: *k3, m1,* repeat around—30 sts total.

Repeat rnds 1 and 2, each time adding an additional k st before the m1, until there are 9 k sts before each m1—66 sts total.

K 2 rnds.

Switch to cn; pm to denote beg/end of rnd.

UNDERSIDE

Rnd 1: *k9, k2tog,* repeat around—60 sts remain.

Rnd 2 and every even rnd: K.

Rnd 3: *k8, k2tog,* repeat around—54 sts remain.

Rnd 5: *k7, k2tog,* repeat around—48 sts remain.

Rnd 6: K 1 rnd.

For *Large* only:

k6, k2tog, repeat around—42 sts remain.

For *Medium* only:

k4, (k2, k2tog) 5x, repeat once more—38 sts remain.

BRIM

K 3 rnds.

BO loosely.

FINISHING

Sew in all ends.

This hat was knit with: Berroco's *Lavish,* 40% nylon/32% wool/15% polyester/13% acrylic, 1³/₄oz/50g = 55yd/50m

Medium (on model)

3 balls, color #7330 (bronzine)

Large

3 balls, color #7335 (malachite)

Note: You will need only a few yards of the third ball of yarn, which means you will have to unwind about 5yd/4.5m and double it up.

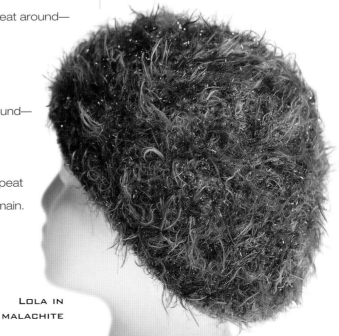

LOLA IN
MALACHITE

BRET

SKILL LEVEL

Beginner

SIZE

Medium
20 to 21"/51 to 53cm

Large
22 to 23"/56 to 58cm

SOME THINGS JUST NEVER CHANGE, AND THANKFULLY THAT OLD ADAGE APPLIES TO THE SIMPLE BERET. THIS PATTERN UPDATES THE CLASSIC VERSION USING THE CHUNKIEST YARN EVER. JUST SLIP IT ON, GIVE IT A SLIGHT TUG TO ONE SIDE, AND OFF YOU GO!

MATERIALS

- Approx 100(110)yd/91(101)m chunky weight yarn
- 6.50mm (size 10½ U.S.) dpn and 24"/61cm cn *or size to obtain gauge*
- Stitch marker
- Darning needle

GAUGE

12 sts = 4"/10cm

Always check gauge.

CROWN

Using dpn, CO 12 sts and divide among 3 dpn *or* do the Wrap Method described on page 14.

Rnd 1 and all odd rnds: K.

Rnd 2: *k1, m1,* repeat around—18 sts total.

Rnd 4: *k2, m1,* repeat around—24 sts total.

Rnd 6: *k3, m1,* repeat around—30 sts total.

Repeat rnds 1 and 2, each time adding an additional k st before each m1, until there are 13(14) k sts before each m1—90(96) sts total.

K 3 rnds.

Switch to cn; pm to denote beg/end of rnd.

UNDERSIDE

Rnd 1: *k13(14), k2tog,* repeat around—84(90) sts remain.

Rnd 2 and all even rnds: K.

Rnd 3: *k12(13), k2tog,* repeat around—78(84) sts remain.

Rnd 5: *k11(12), k2tog,* repeat around—72(78) sts remain.

Rnd 7: *k10(11), k2tog,* repeat around—66(72) sts remain.

Rnd 9: *k9(10), k2tog,* repeat around—60(66) sts remain.

K 3 rnds.

BO loosely.

FINISHING

Sew in all ends.

This hat was knit with: Rowan's *Chunky Print,* 100% wool, 3¹/₂oz/100g = 110yd/100m

Medium and *Large*

1 ball, color #76 (blue multi)

SKILL LEVEL

Experienced

SIZE

Medium
20 to 21"/51 to 53cm

Large
22 to 23"/56 to 58cm

UNLIKE OTHER STYLES IN THIS BOOK,
THIS ENTRELAC BERET IS PROBABLY
NOT ONE THAT YOU ARE GOING TO
KNIT IN THE CAR ON THE WAY TO
THE SKI SLOPES. BUT IF YOU'RE
LOOKING FOR A CHALLENGE, YOUR
EFFORTS WILL BE REWARDED.
ENTRELAC KNITTING CREATES A
BASKET WEAVE EFFECT THAT LOOKS
AS THOUGH THE INDIVIDUAL STRIPS
HAD BEEN KNIT TOGETHER, JUST
LIKE THE LATTICING OF A CHERRY PIE.

MATERIALS

- Approx 120(125)yd/110(114)m chunky weight yarn
- 6½ mm (size 10 1/2 U.S.) dpn and 16"/41cm and 24"/6cm cn *or size to obtain gauge*
- Stitch marker
- Darning needle

GAUGE

12 sts = 4"/10cm

Always check gauge.

CROWN

Using dpn, CO 12 sts and divide among 3 dpn *or* do the Wrap Method described on page 14.

Rnd 1 and all odd rnds: K.

Rnd 2: *k1, m1,* repeat around— 18 sts total.

Rnd 4: *k2, m1,* repeat around— 24 sts total.

Rnd 6: *k3, m1,* repeat around— 30 sts total.

Repeat rnds 1 and 2, each time adding an addtional k st before each m1, until there are 7(8) k sts before each m1— 54(60) sts total.

K 1 rnd, switch to cn (16"/24 for Medium, 24"/61cm for Large); pm to denote beg/end of rnd.

TURN OF CROWN

P 2 rnds.

RISE

(THE BEGINNING OF THE ENTRELAC PATTERN)

Rnd 1 (this rnd makes half-squares or triangles which form the base row):

*k2, turn,

s1, p1, turn,

k3, turn,

s1, p2, turn,

k4, turn,

s1, p3, turn,

k5, turn,

s1, p4, turn,

k6,

Repeat from * to end of round.

Rnd 2: turn, p6 sts just knitted.

Using dpn, **PU 6 sts from edge of square below and p them.

* turn, k6, turn.

Note: PU is to 'pick up' sts; often a dpn is helpful in doing so; also you should not be attaching a ball of yarn, just pick the stitches up in the designated row.

P5, p2tog.

Note: The second stitch of the p2tog comes from the next group of 6 sts on the needle.

Repeat from * 5x more.

Repeat from ** 8(9)x more.

Rnd 3: Turn and k 6 sts just purled.

Using dpn, ** PU 6 sts from the edge of square below and k them

* turn, p6 sts.

K5, skp.

Repeat from * 5x more.

Repeat from ** (8, 9)x more.

Rnd 4: Turn, p 6 sts just knitted.

Using dpn, *PU 6 sts from edge of square below and p them, turn,

k6, turn,

p5, p2tog, turn,

k5, turn,

p4, p2tog, turn,

k4, turn,

p3, p2tog, turn,

k3, turn,

p2, p2tog, turn,

k2, turn,

p1, p3tog,

repeat from ** around.

ELLA IN
ROASTED COFFEE

ELLA IN
FUCHSIA

BRIM

With RS facing, k 7 rnds.

BO loosely.

FINISHING

Sew in all ends.

This hat was knit with: Brown Sheep's *Lamb's Pride Bulky*, 85% wool/15% mohair, 4oz/113g = 125yd/114m

Medium

1 ball, color #M-79 (blue boy)

or

1 ball, color #M-23 (fuchsia)

Large (on model)

1 ball, color #M-16 (seafoam)

or

1 ball, color #M-89 (roasted coffee)

ELLA IN
BLUE BOY

WITTY KNITS

THESE DISTINCTIVE DESIGNS HAVE

ONE THING IN COMMON: THEY'RE FUN—TO MAKE AND TO WEAR. FROM TOPKNOTS TO POM-POMS, TASSELS, EARFLAPS, AND EMBROIDERY, THE HATS IN THIS SECTION OF THE BOOK ALL INCLUDE DELIGHTFUL LITTLE FEATURES THAT MAKE THEM STAND OUT IN A CROWD. YOU'LL LOVE THE COLORS AND TEXTURES OF THE YARNS USED, AND YOU'LL FIND THAT KNITTING THESE SPECIAL DESIGN ELEMENTS IS REALLY QUITE EASY TO DO.

BETH

SKILL LEVEL

Intermediate

SIZE

Medium
20 to 21"/51 to 53cm

Large
22 to 23"/56 to 58cm

THIS TEXTURED CAP FEATURES

TWO KINDS OF TWISTS—
ONE IN THE PATTERN
AND ONE IN THE PLAY-
FUL TOPKNOT.

MATERIALS

- Approx 95(115)yd/87(105)m chunky weight yarn
- 6.50mm (size 10½ U.S.) dpn and 16"/41cm cn *or size to obtain gauge*
- Stitch marker
- Darning needle

GAUGE

12 sts = 4"/10cm

Always check gauge.

BOTTOM EDGE

Using cn, CO 54(60) sts.

P 2 rnds.

RISE

Rnds 1 and 2: *k3, p3,* repeat around.

Rnds 3 and 4: p1, *k3, p3,* repeat around, end p2.

Rnds 5 and 6: p2, *k3, p3,* repeat around, end p1.

Rnds 7 and 8: *p3, k3,* repeat around.

Rnds 9 and 10: k1, *p3, k3,* repeat around, end k2.

Rnds 11 and 12: k2, *p3, k3,* repeat around, end k1.

Repeat rnds 1 through 12 once more.

CROWN

Switch to dpn.

Rnd 1: *k2tog, k1, p3,* repeat around— 45(50) sts remain.

Rnd 2: *k2, p3,* repeat around.

Rnd 3: *k2, p2tog, p1,* repeat around—36(40) sts remain.

Rnds 4 and 5: *k2, p2,* repeat around.

Rnd 6: *k2tog, p2,* repeat around— 27(30) sts remain.

Rnd 7: *k1, p2,* repeat around.

Rnd 8: *k1, p2tog,* repeat around— 18(20) sts remain.

Rnds 9 and 10: *k1, p1,* repeat around.

Rnd 11: k2tog around— 9(10) sts remain.

KNOTTED TOP

K 9(10) sts for 7"/8cm.

K2tog around, then break off the yarn, leaving a 6"/15cm strand; use this strand to thread the remaining stitches with the darning needle; pull tight and fasten.

FINISHING

Sew in all ends and tie the tail at the top of the hat into a knot.

This hat was knit with: Lion Brand's *Kool Wool*, 50% wool/50% acrylic, 1¾oz/50g = 60yd/55m

Medium

2 balls, color #130 (grass)

SKILL LEVEL

Beginner

SIZE

Medium
20 to 21"/51 to 53cm

Large
22 to 23"/56 to 58cm

KRIS

THIS TUBE HAT (PINCHED AT THE TOP)

IS THE QUINTESSENTIAL SLEDDING TOPPER FOR ALL AGES, BUT IN THESE STYLISH COLORS, YOU'RE JUST AS LIKELY TO SEE IT ON A CITY STREET, PAIRED WITH ANYTHING FROM A JEANS JACKET TO A RETRO PUFFER VEST.

MATERIALS

- Color A: Approx 130(150)yd/119(137)m chunky weight yarn
- Color B: Approx 10yd/9m bulky weight yarn
- 5.75mm (size 10 U.S.) 16"/41cm and 24"/61cm cn *or size to obtain gauge*
- Stitch marker
- Darning needle

GAUGE

12 sts = 4"/10cm

Always check gauge.

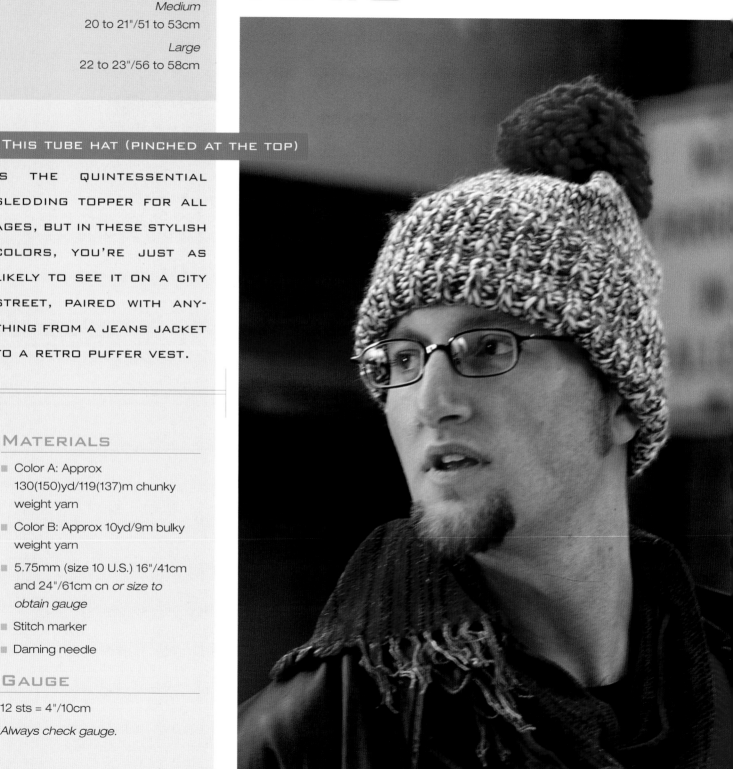

BRIM

Using cn (16"/41cm for Medium, 24"/61cm for Large) and A, CO 56(62) sts.

Pm to denote beg/end of rnd.

K1/p1 rib for 6"/15cm.

RISE

K for 13"/33cm.

BO loosely.

FINISHING

Sew in all ends. Sew the top seam of the hat together by holding the two sides parallel to one another and weave back and forth.

After the hat's top seam has been sewn together, baste the two end-points of the hat together.

With a darning needle and thread, tack down the point where the hat meets to the middle of the hat's top seam. This is the point where the pompom will be attached.

MAKING AND ATTACHING A POMPOM

With B, make a 4"/10cm-diameter pompom according to the instructions on page 29.

This hat was knit with: Rowan's *Chunky Print*, 100% wool, 3½oz/100g = 110yd/100m and Rowan's *Big Wool*, 100% wool, 3½oz/100g = 87yd/80m

Medium (on model)

Color A: 2 balls, Chunky Print, color #75 (swizzle)

Color B: 10yd/9m, Big Wool, color #28 (bohemian)

Beginner

SIZE

Medium

20 to 21"/51 to 53cm

Large

22 to 23"/56 to 58cm

NOTHING COULD BE EASIER TO KNIT

THAN THIS GATHERED-TUBE TOPPER. IT'S A GREAT PATTERN TO USE WITH A VARIETY OF TEXTURED AND PATTERNED YARNS. WHAT SETS IT OFF STYLISTICALLY FROM OTHER "EASY" HATS IS THE TIE (YOUR CHOICE) THAT SERVES TO GATHER THE CROWN TOGETHER.

MATERIALS

- Color A: Approx 160(175)yd/146(160)m heavy worsted weight yarn
- Color B: Approx 30yd/27m heavy worsted weight yarn
- 5.25mm (size 9 U.S.) dpn and 16"/41cm cn *or size to obtain gauge*
- Stitch marker
- Darning needle

GAUGE

16 sts = 4"/10cm

Always check gauge.

BRIM AND RISE

Using cn and A, CO 72(76) sts.

Pm to denote beg/end of rnd.

K for 9½"/24cm.

K2, k2tog, yo, repeat around, end k2(0).

K for 1½"/4cm.

Using B, BO loosely.

FINISHING

Sew in all ends. Using a double strand of B, make a chain 18"/46cm long. Weave this in and out of the yo row, evening out the chain and then securing it with a square knot. Make two 1"/2.5cm pompoms (a quick pompom: wind yarn around two fingers held together and then tie in the middle) and attach to the bottom of the chain.

This hat was knit with: Classic Elite's *Bazic*, 100% wool, 1¾oz/50g = 64yd/59m

Medium

Color A: 2 balls, color #2994 (foliage)

Color B: 1 ball, color #2916 (carnation)

Large (on model)

Color A: 3 balls, color #2919 (impatiens)

Color B: 1 ball, color #2902 (wintergreen)

HEAVY WORSTED
KRINGLE IN FOLIAGE
AND CARNATION

VARIATIONS

For just a little more texture, try one of these tweed chunky weight yarns.

MATERIALS

- Color A: Approx 109(135)yd/ 98(123)m chunky weight yarn
- Color B: Approx 30yd/27m chunky weight yarn
- 5.75mm (size 10 U.S.) dpn and 16"/41cm cn *or size to obtain gauge*
- Stitch marker
- Darning needle

GAUGE

12 sts = 4"/10cm

Always check gauge.

BRIM AND RISE

Using cn and color A, CO 60 (64) sts.

Pm to denote beg/end of rnd.

K for 9½"/24cm.

K2, k2tog, yo, repeat around.

K for 1½"/4cm.

Using a double strand (3yd/3m long) of color B, BO loosely.

FINISHING

Sew in all ends. Using a double strand of color B, make a chain 18"/46cm long. Weave this in and out of the yo row, evening out the chain and then securing it with a square knot. Make two 1"/2.5cm pompoms (a quick pompom: wind yarn around two fingers held together and then tie in the middle) and attach to the bottom of the chain.

This hat was knit with: Rowan's *Yorkshire Tweed Chunky*, 100% wool, 3½oz/100g = 123yd/113m and Rowan's *Yorkshire Tweed DK*, 100% wool, 1¾oz/50g = 123yd/113m

Medium

Color A: 2 balls, *Tweed Chunky*, color #556 (flaming)

Color B: 1 ball, *Tweed DK*, color #347 (skip)

Large

Color A: 2 balls, *Tweed Chunky*, color #550 (damp)

Color B: 1 ball, *Tweed DK*, color #344 (scarlet)

CHUNKY WEIGHT
KRINGLE IN DAMP
AND SCARLET

CHUNKY WEIGHT
KRINGLE IN FLAMING
AND SKIP

POPPY

SKILL LEVEL

Beginner

SIZE

Medium
20 to 21"/51 to 53cm

Large
22 to 23"/56 to 58cm

A RIBBED CAP IS A CHEERFUL ALTERNATIVE

FOR THE SLOPES OR YOUR NEXT SNOWMAN BUILDING ADVENTURE. THIS HAT HAS THE SAME FORM AS KRINGLE (PAGE 114), BUT VARIATIONS ARE ADDED EVERY STEP ALONG THE WAY. MAKE ALL THE POMPOMS THE SAME, OR EACH IN A DIFFERENT COLOR. ADD AN EXTRA JINGLE BY SEWING A SIMPLE BELL INTO THE CORE OF EACH POMPOM.

MATERIALS

- Color A: 32(35)yd/29(32)m heavy worsted weight yarn
- Color B: 32(35)yd/29(32)m heavy worsted weight yarn
- Color C: 32(35)yd/29(32)m heavy worsted weight yarn
- Color D: 32(35)yd/29(32)m heavy worsted weight yarn
- Color E: 32(35)yd/29(32)m heavy worsted weight yarn
- 3yd/3m of extra yarn in the three colors for the pompoms
- 5.25mm (size 9 U.S.) dpn and 16"/41cm cn *or size to obtain gauge*
- Stitch marker
- Darning needle

GAUGE

16 sts = 4"/10cm

Always check gauge.

BRIM AND RISE

Using cn and A, CO 72 (80) sts.

Pm to denote beg/end of rnd.

K2, p2, repeat around.

K2/p2, for 13"/33cm, changing colors every 5th row.

BO loosely in k2/p2 rib.

FINISHING

Sew in all ends. The bottom 3"/7.6 cm will be turned upward to form the brim, so weave ends in on the front side, then turn edge up.

POMPOMS

Using three 1½"/4cm-diameter pompoms in the colors of your choice according to the instructions on page 29. Place the pompoms in equidistant positions at the top edge of the hat by attaching three safety pins at equidistant positions around the edge of the hat. Then bring the three pins together and baste a knot in the center to hold the hat together. Using a darning needle threaded with yarn, attach the pompoms in the three separate folds created by the center-basted folds.

This hat was knit with: Classic Elite's *Montera*, 50% llama/50% wool, 3½oz/100g = 127yd/116m

Medium and *Large* (on model)

Color A: 1 ball, color #3856 (majolica blue)

Color B: 1 ball, color #3831 (turquoise)

Color C: 1 ball, color #3893 (ch'ulla blue)

Color D: 1 ball, color #2850 (glade green)

Color E: 1 ball, color #3832 (puma magenta)

VARIATION

Try knitting this hat with no stripes using Classic Elite's *Montera,* 50% llama/50% wool, 3½oz/100g = 127yd/116m.

Medium and *Large*

Color A: 2 balls, color #3893 (ch'ulla blue)

Color B: 4yd/4m, color #3832 (puma magenta)

Color C: 4yd/4m, color #3831 (turquoise)

Color D: 4yd/4m, color #3856 (majolica blue)

POPPY IN CH'ULLA BLUE, PUMA MAGENTA, TURQUOISE AND MAJOLICA BLUE

SKILL LEVEL

Intermediate

SIZE

Medium
20 to 21"/51 to 53cm

Large
22 to 23"/56 to 58cm

MIKA

WHAT WOULD A TRENDSETTING ELF WEAR?

A BIG-TEXTURED, RIBBED, CONICAL CAP WITH A CONTRASTING POMPOM IN A SNAPPY COLOR LIKE THIS ONE. IT'S CHEERFUL AND A BIT CHEEKY. WE DARE YOU TO TRY TO STAY IN A BAD MOOD WHEN YOU WEAR IT.

MATERIALS

- Color A: Approx 110(115)yd/ 101(105)m bulky weight yarn
- Color B: Approx 5yd/5m bulky weight yarn
- 8mm (size 11 U.S.) dpn and 24"/61cm cn *or size to obtain gauge*
- Stitch marker
- Darning needle

GAUGE

10 sts = 4"/10cm

Always check gauge.

BRIM AND RISE

Using cn and A, CO 48 (52) sts.

Pm to denote beg/end of rnd.

Work k2/p2 rib for 9"/23cm.

Rnd 1: *k2, p2tog,* repeat around—36(39) sts total.

Rnd 2: *k2, p1,* repeat around.

Switch to dpn.

Rnd 3: *k2tog, p1,* repeat around—24(26) sts total.

Rnd 4: *k1, p1,* repeat around.

Rnd 5: k2tog around—12(13) sts total.

Rnd 6: *k2tog,* repeat around, end k 0,(1)—6(7) sts total.

Without binding off, cut the yarn so that there is an 8"/20cm tail. Thread the tail onto a darning needle and pull through every remaining stitch. Tie off.

FINISHING

Sew in all ends. With B, make a 6˝/15cm-diameter loose pompom according to the instructions on page 29. Attach the pompom to the top of the crown.

This hat was knit with: Brown Sheep's *Burley Spun,* 100% wool, 8 oz/226g = 132yd/121m

Medium

Color A: 1 ball, color #BS155 (lemon drop)

Color B: 5yd/5m, color #BS68 (pine tree)

OR

Color A: 1 ball, color #BS10 (cream)

Color B: 5 yd/5m each, colors #BS68 (pine tree), #BS120 (limeade) and #BS165 (Christmas green)

Large (on model)

Color A: 1 ball, color #BS120 (limeade)

Color B: 5 yd/5m, color #BS155 (lemon drop)

OR

Color A: 1 ball, color #BS68 (pine tree)

Color B: 5yd/5m, color #BS115 (oatmeal)

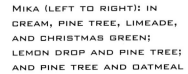

MIKA (LEFT TO RIGHT): IN CREAM, PINE TREE, LIMEADE, AND CHRISTMAS GREEN; LEMON DROP AND PINE TREE; AND PINE TREE AND OATMEAL

COSIMA

SKILL LEVEL

Intermediate

SIZE

Medium
20 to 21"/51 to 53cm

Large
22 to 23"/56 to 58cm

FEATURING SUBTLY TEXTURED STRIPES

AND LUXURIOUSLY SOFT WOOL, COSIMA IS A VERSATILE CHOICE. IT'S WHIMSICAL ENOUGH TO WEAR WITH JEANS, BUT WOULDN'T LOOK OUT OF PLACE WITH A DRESSY COAT.

MATERIALS

- Color A: 100(110)yd/91(101)m chunky weight yarn
- Color B: 40(40)yd/37(37)m chunky weight yarn
- 5.25mm (size 9 U.S.) dpn and 16"/41cm cn *or size to obtain gauge*
- Stitch marker
- Darning needle

GAUGE

13 sts = 4"/10cm

Always check gauge.

CROWN

Using dpn and A, CO 12 sts and among between 3 dpn *or* do the Wrap Method described on page 14.

Rnd 1 and all odd rnds: K.

Rnd 2: *k1, m1,* repeat around— 18 sts total.

Rnd 4: *k2, m1,* repeat around— 24 sts total.

Rnd 6: *k3, m1,* repeat around— 30 sts total.

Repeat rnds 1 and 2, each time adding an additional k st before each m1, until there are 10(11) k sts before each m1— 72(78) sts total.

K 1 rnd.

Switch to cn; pm to denote beg/end of rnd.

TURN OF CROWN

P 3 rnds.

RISE

K 2 rnds.

With B: P 2 rnds.

With A: K 3 rnds.

Repeat the last 5 rnds, 4x more.

With A: K 2 rnds.

P 2 rnds

BO 7(9), p16(17) place on dpn, for earflap, BO 26 (26), p16(17) place on dpn, for earflap, BO7(9).

EARFLAPS

With RS facing and working back and forth on dpn, attach A:

Row 1: k3, p10(11), k3.

Row 2: p3, k10(11), p3.

Rows 3 and 4: Repeat rows 1 and 2.

Row 5: k3, p2tog, p6(7), p2tog, k3.

Row 6: p3, k8(9), p3.

Row 7: k3, p2tog, p4(5), p2tog, k3.

Row 8: p3, k6(7), p3.

Row 9: k3, p2tog, p2(3), p2tog, k3.

Row 10: p3, k4(5), p3.

Row 11: k3, p2tog, p0(1), p2tog, k3.

Row 12: p3, k2tog(k3tog), p3.

Row 13: K.

Row 14: p1, p2tog, p1, p2tog, p1.

Row 15: k2tog, k1, BO, k2tog, BO.

Draw a string through the remaining st and fasten off.

FINISHING

Sew in all ends.

With B, make two tassels (see page 29) and sew them to the ends of the earflaps.

This hat was knit with: Tahki Stacy Charles' *Bunny,* 50% wool/25% alpaca/25% acrylic, 1³⁄₄oz/50g = 81yd/89m

Medium (on model)

Color A: 2 balls, color #5 (mint green)

Color B: 1 ball, color #4 (soft pink)

Large

Color A: 2 balls, color #13 (rust)

Color B: 1 ball, color #3 (gray)

COSIMA IN RUST
AND GRAY

SKILL LEVEL

Intermediate

SIZE

Medium
20 to 21"/51 to 53cm

Large
22 to 23"/56 to 58cm

THIS SKIRTED HELMET PREPARES YOU

TO BATTLE EVEN THE ICIEST OF STORMS
IN STYLE. IF YOU'RE A SPORTS FAN, MAKE
THE STRIPES IN COLORS TO HONOR YOUR
FAVORITE TEAM.

MATERIALS

- Color A: Approx 100(105)yd/91(96)m chunky weight yarn
- Color B: Approx 10yd/9m chunky weight yarn
- Color C: Approx 10yd/9m chunky weight yarn
- Color D: Approx 15yd/14m chunky weight yarn
- 5.75mm (size 10 U.S.) dpn and 16"/41cm and 24"/61cm cn *or size to obtain gauge*
- Stitch marker
- Darning needle

GAUGE

14 sts = 4"/10 cm

Always check gauge.

SKYE IN BURGUNDY,
DARK GRAY HEATHER,
LIGHT GRAY HEATHER
AND BLACK

CROWN

Using dpn and A, CO 12 sts and divide among 3 dpn, *or* do the Wrap Method described on page 14.

Rnd 1 and all odd rnds: K.

Rnd 2: *k1, m1,* repeat around—18 sts total.

Rnd 4: *k2, m1,* repeat around—24 sts total.

Rnd 6: *k3, m1,* repeat around—30 sts total.

Repeat rnds 1 and 2, each time adding an additional k st before each m1, until there are 9(10) k sts before each m1—66(72) sts total.

K 1 rnd.

Switch to cn (16"/41cm for *Medium,* 14"/61cm for *Large*); pm to denote beg/end of rnd.

TURN OF CROWN

P 3 rnds.

RISE

With A, k 2 rnds.

With B, k 2 rnds.

With C, k 1 rnd.

With D, k 5 rnds.

With C, k 1 rnd.

With B, k 2 rnds.

With A, k 2 rnds.

Note: The next round ensures that the color changes occur at the back of the hat.

Using A, for 3 rnds: k19(21), p28(30), k 19(21) to end.

K19(21), p3, BO the next 22(24) sts by purling, p2, k19(21).

Remove marker, (indicating mid-point of remaining stitches) k to the last 3 sts, p3.

Note: Now that you're at end of row, begin to work back and forth to create the lower flap.

EARFLAP AND HEADFLAP

Work back and forth on cn (16"/41 for Medium, 14"/61cm for large);

S1, k2, p to last 3 sts, k3.

S1, p2, k to last 3 sts, p3.

Repeat the last two rows for 2"/5cm. End with a p row.

S1, k to end.

S1, p to end.

BO loosely.

FINISHING

Sew in all ends.

This hat was knit with: JCA Reynolds' *Lopi,* 100% wool, 3½oz/100g = 110yd/100m

Medium

Color A: 1 ball, color #116 (burgundy)

Color B: 10yd/9m color #57 (dark heather gray)

Color C: 10yd/9m color #54 (light heather gray)

Color D: 15yd/14m, color #59 (black)

Large (on model)

Color A: 1 ball, color #54 (light heather gray)

Color B: 10yd/9m, color #59 (black)

Color C: 10yd/9m, color 57 (dark heather gray)

Color D: 15yd/14m, color #116 (burgundy)

VARIATION

Embroider flowers around the rise using a lazy daisy stitch (see page 28), then add French knots to the centers for a more feminine look. In addition to the yarns listed, you'll need scraps of yarn in different colors for embroidering the flowers.

This hat was knit with: JCA Reynolds' *Lopi,* 100% wool, 3½oz/100g = 110yd/100m

Medium

Color A: 1 ball, color #378 (green)

Color B: 15yd/14m, color #168 (burgundy)

Color C: 30yd/27m, color #910 (fuchsia)

Large

Color A: 1 ball, color #432 (medium lavender)

Color B: 15yd/14m, color #168 (green)

Color C: 30yd/27m, color #910 (dark purple)

Color D: 15yd/14m, color #214 (aqua)

SKYE (LEFT TO RIGHT): IN GREEN, BURGUNDY, AND FUCHSIA, AND MEDIUM LAVENDER, GREEN, DARK PURPLE AND AQUA

HILDA

SKILL LEVEL
Intermediate

SIZE
Medium
20 to 21"/51 to 53cm

Large
22 to 23"/56 to 58cm

> THIS LOVABLE HELMETED HAT
>
> WITH POMPOM-TIPPED FLAPS
> IS GREAT FUN TO MAKE AND
> WEAR. USE BRIGHT COLORS
> FOR AN IRRESISTIBLY CHEER-
> FUL LOOK.

MATERIALS

- Color A: Approx 60(63)yd/55(57)m bulky weight yarn
- Color B: Approx 60(63)yd/55(57)m bulky weight yarn
- Color C (for pompoms): Approx 3yd/3m bulky weight yarn
- 8mm (size 11 U.S.) dpn and 16"/41 cm and 24"/61cm cn *or size to obtain gauge*
- Stitch marker
- Darning needle

GAUGE

10 sts = 4"/10cm

Always check gauge.

CROWN

Using dpn and A, CO 12 sts and among between 3 dpn *or* do the Wrap Method described on page 14.

Rnd 1 and all odd rnds: K.

Rnd 2: *k1, m1,* repeat around—18 sts total.

Rnd 4: *k2, m1,* repeat around—24 sts total.

Rnd 6: *k3, m1,* repeat around—30 sts total.

Repeat rnds 1 and 2, each time adding an additonal k st before each m1, until there are 6(7) k sts before each m1—48(54) sts total.

K 1 rnd.

Switch to 16"/41cm cn; pm to denote beg/end of rnd.

K23(26), m1, repeat once more—50(56) sts total.

RISE

K 2(0) rnds.

Switch to B, k 1 rnd.

Using 24"/61cm cn, continue to knit back and forth (garter stitch)—not in the rnd—creating a split in the back of the hat for 8"/20cm, from top of crown, ending with a WS rnd.

With RS facing, BO (6, 6), sts, k11(13) and place the 12(14) sts worked on holder or dpn (first earflap), BO 14(16), k11(13) sts and place the 12(14) sts worked on holder or dpn (first earflap), BO (6, 6) sts.

EARFLAPS

With WS facing and using B, k 2 rows.

On the next row, k2tog, k to end.

Repeat last row until there are only 2 sts left, k2tog.

Leave a 10˝/22cm tail to be used to attach the pompoms to the earflap ends.

FINISHING

Sew back seam and sew in all ends.

With C (and D if you want different colors for each pompoms), make 2½"/4cm-diameter pompoms according to the instructions on page 29 and attach to earflap ends.

HILDA (LEFT TO RIGHT): IN FUCHSIA, ORANGE YOU GLAD, AND LIMEADE; CHARCOAL HEATHER, FUCHSIA, LEMON DROP, AND ORANGE YOU GLAD; AND CHRISTMAS GREEN, BLUE BOY, LIMEADE, AND FUCHSIA

This hat was knit with: Brown Sheep's *Burley Spun*, 100% wool, 8oz/226g = 132yd/121m

Medium

Color A: 1 ball, color #BS165 (Christmas green)

Color B: 1 ball, color #BS79 (blue boy)

Color C: 3yd/3m, color #BS120 (limeade)

Color D: 3yd/3 m color #BS23 (fuchsia)

or

Color A: 1 ball, color #BS23 (fuchsia)

Color B: 1 ball, color #BS110 (orange you glad)

Color C: 3yd/3m, color #BS120 (limeade)

Large

Color A: 1 ball, color #BS04 (charcoal heather)

Color B: 1 ball, color #BS23 (fuchsia)

Color C: 3yd/3m color # BS155 (lemon drop)

Color D: 3yd/3m, color #BS110 (orange you glad)

Or (on model)

Color A: 1 ball, color #BS79 (blue boy)

Color B: 1 ball, color #BS165 (Christmas green)

Color C: 3yd/3m, color #BS120 (limeade)

FABULOUS FELTED

WHO CAN RESIST THE LUSCIOUS

TEXTURE OF FELTED WOOL? IT'S EASY TO
TRANSFORM YOUR KNITTED HAT INTO A FELTED
ONE USING A FEW SIMPLE TECHNIQUES YOU
CAN LEARN ABOUT ON PAGES 18 TO 21. THE
PATTERNS IN THIS SECTION ARE PERFECT FOR
FELTING, RESULTING IN CHARMING HATS THAT
ARE AS WARM AS THEY ARE CHIC. FELTED
EMBELLISHMENTS ADD PANACHE TO YOUR
HAT WITHOUT MUCH EXTRA TIME OR EFFORT.

SKILL LEVEL

Intermediate

SIZE

Medium
20 to 21"/51 to 53cm
Large
22 to 23"/56 to 58cm

THIS FELTED BUCKET HAT

IS CASUALLY STYLED, BUT STILL COMES ACROSS AS DIGNIFIED AND ATTRACTIVE—A GREAT MATE FOR ANY JACKET AND EVEN A MORE FORMAL COAT. JUST ABOUT ANY MOHAIR YARN WITH MOHAIR CONTENT OF 75 PERCENT OR GREATER WILL WORK FOR THIS HAT; HOWEVER, FEW MOHAIR YARNS COMPARE TO THE CREAMY TEXTURE OF CAPRICORN MOHAIR, STRAIGHT FROM THE BRITISH COUNTRYSIDE.

MATERIALS

- Color A: Approx 110(120)yd/ 101(110)m chunky weight wool yarn
- Color B: Approx 110(120)yd/ 101(110)m chunky weight mohair yarn
- Scraps of yarn for leaves
- 6.5mm (size 10½ U.S.) dpn and 24"/61cm cn *or size to obtain gauge*
- Stitch marker
- Darning needle

GAUGE

10 sts (with A and B together) = 4"/10cm

Always check gauge.

CROWN

Using dpn and A and B together, CO 12 sts and divide them among 3 dpn *or* do the Wrap Method described on page 14.

Rnd 1 and all odd rnds: K.

Rnd 2: *k1, m1,* repeat around— 18 sts total.

Rnd 4: *k2, m1,* repeat around— 24 sts total.

Rnd 6: *k3, m1,* repeat around— 30 sts total.

Repeat rnds 1 and 2, each time adding an additional k before each m1 until there are 9(10) sts before each m1— 66(72) sts total.

K 1 rnd.

Switch to cn; pm to denote beg/end of rnd.

P 3 rnds.

RISE

K for 4½(5)"/12(13)cm.

BRIM

K3, m1, repeat around, ending k2(0).

K 5 rnds.

BO loosely.

FINISHING

Sew in all ends. Follow the felting instructions on pages 19 to 21 to felt the hat.

Knit and felt the embellishments according to the instructions on pages 19 to 21.

This hat was knit with: Reynold's *Lopi,* 100% Wool, 3½oz/100g = 110yd/100m and Capricorn's *Mohair,* 82% mohair/9% wool/9% nylon, 1½oz/50g = 100yd/100m

Medium (on model)
Color A: 1 ball, color #6570 (jade green)
Color B: 1 ball, color #6502 (gold leaf)

or
Color A: 1 ball, Lopi, color #59 (black)
Color B: 2 balls, Mohair, color #121 (black)

EMMA (LEFT TO RIGHT): IN BLACK; IN MEDIUM AND LIGHT GRAY; IN LIGHT GRAY; AND IN MEDIUM AND LIGHT GRAY

VARIATION

To make the two-toned version, you will need to purchase two different colors of mohair. Complete the pattern to 1½"/4cm beyond the turn of crown. Break off the first mohair color and attach the second mohair color and finish completing the pattern.

Large (on background model)

Color A: 2 balls, *Lopi*, color #58 (medium gray)

Color B: 2 balls *Mohair*, color #132 (medium gray) and #160 (light gray)

CLEM

SKILL LEVEL

Intermediate

SIZE

Medium
20 to 21"/51 to 53cm
Large
22 to 23"/56 to 58cm

DARLING CLEM FEATURES AN UPTURNED BRIM THAT'S PERFECT FOR EMBROIDERY. USE YARNS IN COMPLEMENTARY AND CONTRASTING COLORS FOR A DESIGN THAT REALLY STANDS OUT.

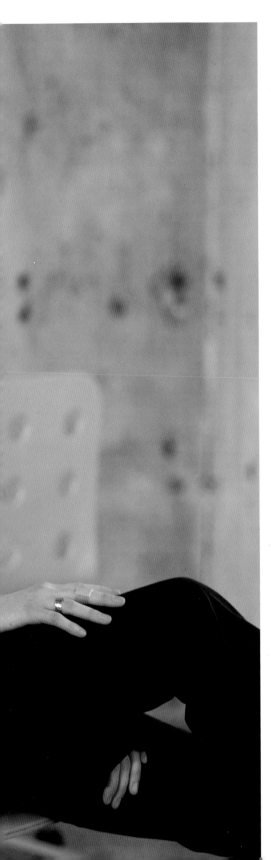

MATERIALS

- Color A: Approx 110(120)yd/ 101(110)m bulky weight yarn
- Color B: Approx 110(120)yd/ 101(110)m bulky weight yarn
- 6.5mm (size 10½ U.S.) dpn and 16"/41cm and 24"/61cm cn *or size to obtain gauge*
- Scraps of wool for embroidery
- Stitch marker
- Darning needle

GAUGE

10 sts (with A and B together) = 4"/10cm

Always check gauge.

CROWN

Using dpn and holding a strand A and B, CO 12 sts and divide between 3 dpn *or* do the Wrap Method described on page 14 to obtain the initial 12 sts.

Rnd 1 and all odd rnds: K.

Rnd 2: *k1, m1,* repeat around— 18 sts total.

Rnd 4: *k2, m1,* repeat around— 24 sts total.

Rnd 6: *k3, m1,* repeat around— 30 sts total.

Repeat rnds 1 and 2, each time adding an additional k st before each m1, until there are 9(10) k sts before each m1— 66(72) sts total.

Switch to cn (16"/41cm for Medium and 24"/61cm for Large); pm to denote the beg/end of rnd.

RISE

K until piece measures 8½(9)"/23(24)cm from top of crown.

BRIM

K2, m1, repeat around.

Turn work, and beginning to work with WS facing, k for 4"/10cm.

BO loosely.

FINISHING

Sew in all ends.

Felt the hat according to the instructions on page 19 to 21. When shaping it after laundering, pull out the brim and then push the front brim upwards.

See page 28 for instructions on how to embroider flowers on the upturned brim.

This hat was knit with: JCA Reynold's *Lopi,* 100% wool, 3½oz/100g = 110yd/100m and Capricorn's *Mohair,* 82% mohair/9% wool/9% nylon, 1¾oz/50g = 110yd/100m

Medium (on model)

Color A: 2 balls, *Lopi,* color #209 (rose)

Color B:2 balls, *mohair,* color #104 (cerise)

CESCA

SKILL LEVEL

Intermediate

SIZE

Medium
20 to 21"/51 to 53cm
Large
22 to 23"/56 to 58cm

THIS FELTED, BRIMMED, BUCKET HAT

IS CASUALLY STYLED, YET SOPHISTICATED. WHAT MAKES THIS PARTICULAR DESIGN INTERESTING IS THAT THE EYE-LASH STRIPING IS ACRYLIC, AND THEREFORE RESISTS THE FELTING PROCESS, CREATING ITS OWN INTERESTING PATTERN WITHIN THE FELTED WOOL.

MATERIALS

- Color A: Approx 110(120)yd/ 101(110)m chunky weight yarn
- Color B: Approx 110(120)yd/101(110)m eyelash yarn
- 6.5mm (size 10½ U.S.) dpn and 16"/41cm and 24"/61cm cn *or size to obtain gauge*
- Stitch marker
- Darning needle

GAUGE

10 sts = 4"/10cm

Always check gauge.

CROWN

Using dpn and A, CO 12 sts and divide among 3 dpn *or* do the Wrap Method described on page 14.

Rnd 1 and all odd rnds: K.

Rnd 2: *k1, m1,* repeat around—18 sts total.

Starting with rnd 3 and for the next two rnds, attach a strand of eyelash yarn, and k it together with the wool. Repeat for every alternate 3 rnds thereafter.

Note: There is no need to cut the eyelash strand. When not in use, just let it hang in the back. During the felting process it gets woven into the hat structure.

Rnd 4: *k2, m1,* repeat around—24 sts total.

Rnd 6: *k3, m1,* repeat around—30 sts total.

Repeat rnds 1 and 2, each time adding an additional k st before each m1 until there are 9(10) k sts before each m1—66(72) sts total.

K1 rnd.

Switch to cn (16"/41cm for Medium, 24"/61cm for Large); pm to denote the beg/end of rnd.

TURN OF CROWN

P 3 rnds.

RISE

Continue knitting with A and B together every 3 rnds:

k for 4(4½)"/10(11)cm.

BRIM

With A only, k 1 rnd.

K3, m1, repeat around, ending k2(0).

K 5 rnds.

With A and B together, k 1 rnd.

BO loosely.

FINISHING

Sew in all ends. Follow the felting instructions on page 19 to 21 to felt the hat.

This hat was knit with: Brown Sheep's *Lamb's Pride Bulky,* 85% wool/15% mohair, 4oz/113g = 125yd/114m and Bernat's *Boa,* 100% polyester, 1¾oz/50g = 71yd/65m

Medium (on model)

Color A: 1 ball, *Lamb's Pride Bulky,* color #M-23 (fuchsia)

Color B: 1 ball, *Boa,* color #81505 (phoenix)

Large

Color A: 1 ball, *Lamb's Pride Bulky,* color #M-175 (bronze patina)

Color B: 1 ball, *Boa,* color #81040 (raven)

CESCA IN BRONZE
PATINA AND RAVEN

LYDIA

SKILL LEVEL

Intermediate

SIZE

Medium
20 to 21"/51 to 53cm

Large
22 to 23"/56 to 58cm

THIS ROUNDED-CROWN AND FLARED-BRIM

FELTED TOPPER LOOKS GREAT WHEN THE COLLAR OF THE WEARER'S COAT OR JACKET IS UPTURNED AS WELL. ALTHOUGH CHARMING IF WORN PLAIN, IT ALSO BEGS FOR AN ORNAMENT—A FELTED FLOWER OR A LARGE VINTAGE BROOCH—TO COMPLETE THE PICTURE.

MATERIALS

- Color A: Approx 110(120)yd/101(110)m mohair chunky weight yarn
- Color B: Approx 110(120)yd/101(110)m wool chunky weight yarn
- 6.50mm (size 10½ U.S.) dpn and 24"/61cm cn *or size to obtain gauge*
- Stitch marker
- Darning needle

GAUGE

10 sts (with A and B together) = 4"/10cm

Always check gauge.

CROWN

Using dpn and holding a strand of A and B together, CO 12 sts and divide among 3 dpn *or* do the Wrap Method described on page 14.

Rnd 1 and all odd rnds: K.

Rnd 2: *k1, m1,* repeat around— 18 sts total.

Rnd 4: *k2, m1,* repeat around— 24 sts total.

Rnd 6: *k3, m1,* repeat around— 30 sts total.

Repeat rnds 1 and 2, each time adding an additional k st before each m1, until there are 9(10) k sts before each m1— 66(72) sts.

Switch to cn; pm to denote beg/end of rnd.

K for 11(11½)"/28(29)cm from top of crown.

BRIM

K3, m1, repeat around, ending k2(0).

K6 rnds.

BO loosely.

FINISHING

Sew in all ends. Follow the felting instructions on page 19 to 21 to felt the hat.

This hat was knit with: Capricorn's *Mohair*, 82% mohair/9%wool/9% nylon, 1¾oz/50g = 110yd/100m and JCA Reynold's *Lopi*, 100% wool, 3½oz/100g = 110yd/100m

Medium

Color A: 2 balls, Mohair, color #154 (sea green)

Color B: 2 balls, Lopi, color #0308 (sea green)

Large (on model)

Color A: 2 balls, Mohair, color #129 (turquoise)

Color B: 2 balls, Lopi, color #0214 (turquoise)

LYDIA IN
SEA GREEN

SOPHIE

A FELTED PILLBOX CAN LOOK LADYLIKE OR RETRO-FABULOUS. CUSTOMIZE IT WITH FELTED APPLIQUÉ OR A SMALL VINTAGE PIN FOR ADDED PIZZAZZ. LIKE THE LYDIA (SEE PAGE 140), SOPHIE LOOKS PARTICULARLY SNAZZY WITH AN EMBELLISHMENT OFF TO THE SIDE.

MATERIALS

- Color A: Approx 105(108)yds/96(109)m heavy worsted weight yarn
- Color B: Approx 105(108)yds/96(109)m chunky weight yarn
- 6.50mm (size 10½ US) dpn and 24"/61cm cn *or size to obtain gauge*
- Stitch marker
- Darning needle

GAUGE

10 sts (with A and B together) = 4"/10cm

Always check gauge.

CROWN

Using dpn and with A and B together, CO 12 sts and divide among 3 dpn *or* do the Wrap Method described on page 14.

Rnd 1 and all odd rnds: K.

Rnd 2: *k1, m1,* repeat around— 18 sts total.

Rnd 4: *k2, m1,* repeat around— 24 sts total.

Rnd 6: *k3, m1,* repeat around— 30 sts total.

Repeat rnds 1 and 2, each time adding an additional k st before each m1, until there are 9(10) k sts before each m1— 66(72) sts total.

K 1 rnd.

Switch to cn; pm to denote beg/end of rnd.

TURN OF CROWN

P 3 rnds.

RISE

K for 4 1/2(4 3/4)"/11(12)cm.

TURN OF CROWN

P 3 rnds.

Turn, working on the WS, BO loosely.

FINISHING

Sew in ends. Felt the hat according the instructions on page 19 to 21.

This hat was knit with: Capricorn's *Mohair,* 82% mohair/9%wool/9% nylon, 1 3/4oz/50g = 110yd/100m, JCA Reynold's *Lopi,* 100% wool, 3 1/2oz/100g, 110yd/100m

Medium (on model)

Color A: 1 ball, *Mohair,* color #141 (blue)

Color B: 1 ball, *Lopi,* color #9 (blue)

Large

Color A: 1 ball, *Mohair,* color #141 (green)

Color B: 1 ball, *Lopi,* color #378 (green)

SOPHIE IN
GREEN

Notes About Suppliers

Usually, the supplies you need for making the projects in Lark books can be found at your local craft supply store, discount mart, home improvement center, or retail shop relevant to the topic of the book. Occasionally, however, you may need to buy materials or tools from specialty suppliers. In order to provide you with the most up-to-date information, we have created a listing of suppliers on our Web site, which we update on a regular basis. Visit us at www.larkbooks.com, click on "Craft Supply Sources," and then click on the relevant topic. You will find numerous companies listed with their web address and/or mailing address and phone number.

Acknowledgments

Special thanks goes out to:

Doris Erb of Bernat

Deanna Gavioli of Berocco

Linda Niemeyer of Blue Sky Alpacas

Judy Wilson of
Brown Sheep Company

Rita and Mike Collins of Capricorn Yarns

Judy Croucher, Pat Chew, and
Kathy Lacher of Classic Elite Yarns

Susan Mills of JCA/Reynolds

Stephanie Klose of Lion Brand Yarns

Joelle Rioux of Rowan

Deborah Errico of
Tahki-Stacy Charles, Inc.

Give credit where it's due!!

Capricorn Yarns' correct name is Capricorn Mohair Ltd—this is a British farm/firm that produces gorgeous mohair—do check out their line: www.capricorn-mohair.com. Importing from Britain is just as easy as ordering domestically in the USA.

Index